«The sooner you let go»

Green Wallpaper !

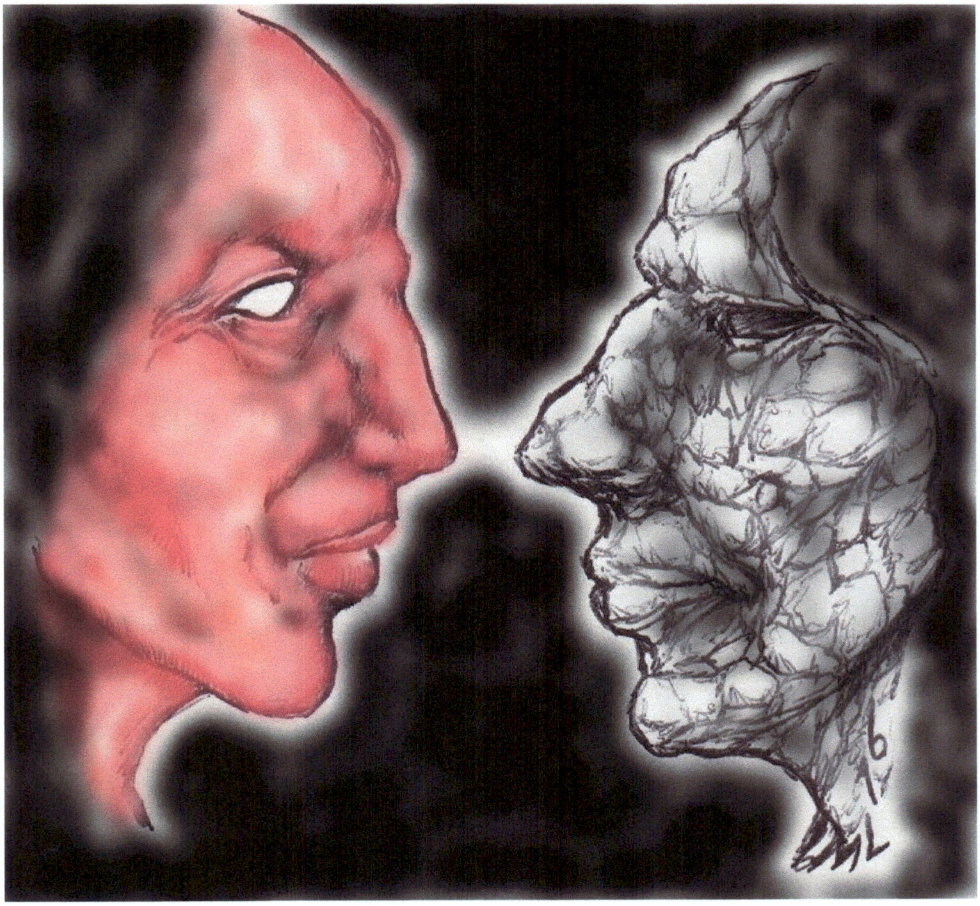

The sooner you let go,
and give, and take in,
breathe, move away,
enjoy peace, and give in,
take yourself in your arms,
and hold back, and walk around,
and be silent,
hear the sounds,
the rattling of the bones,
the trembling inside you,
that shakes you,
the waterfall that protects you,
the words that are written on your skin.
The sooner he will look you in the eyes again!

Wir haben von Tausenden von Jahren
bis heute einen langen Weg zurückgelegt. Wir sollten uns als Menschen,
denen ihr Ego gehört, entscheiden, unsere Umwelt selbst im schlimmsten
Beispiel, das terrestrische Bürger jemals getan haben, zu entwickeln.
Vielleicht sollten wir alle darüber nachdenken, welchen Weg wir gehen, und
unsere älteren Menschen tragen und die Schöpfer werden, die unseren
Kindern eine sichere Zukunft garantieren !

Vi har kommit långt från tusentals år till idag.
Vi som människor som äger sina egon bör välja att utveckla vår miljö,
sett även i det värsta exemplet markbundna medborgare
någonsin har gjort. Kanske borde vi alla tänka på vilken väg
vi ska gå och våra äldre ska bära och bli skaparna
som garanterar våra barn en säker framtid !

We were going a long way from thousands of years, until today.
We should decide as humans that own their ego to develop our environment
even in the worst example that terrestrian citizans ever did, so we should
maybe all start to think to what way we decide to go, and carrie our elderly
become those creators that guarantee our kid a save future !

Heike Thieme

Hinter Mauern scheint es violett

さん〜素敵ですね〜

DU BIST WUNDERBAR

Heike Thieme !

Go out in nature
sit down on a bench,
breathing in and out,
watching the birds,
see the leaves in the trees,
them moving through the wind,
ending the day with it,
took this in your heart,
pushed all thought away,
with a cloud, passing on,
ended the day, as if you reached your aim,
did what you could do,
the whole plunder, absurdity and doubts gone,
passed with the clouds and dissappeared,
tomorrow will be another day,
tomorrow will be another day,
and you see it in a vision,
in awareness of your high spirituality,
within your powers sending out,
you see it in a dream,
what strong child lives in you,
that puts your crone on the head
the one that you earned !

The German philosopher
(Immanuel Kant) was asked:
What is the difference between
law and morality?

He answered:
In law: a person is guilty
when he violates the rights of others.
In morality: a person is guilty
if he thinks about it.

« Heike Thieme »

Since more than 30 years,
here the people are not so nice,
but in a province is more envy and greed,
the envy of my kindfulness, and the greed,
that i might own heartfeeling richdom
more than the usual people.
Yes, they are nice, you can find them sitting alone.

Without a future - no future
a little tree on the left, a little tree on the right,
and you still dare to dream, standing in front of the trees,
and looking up to the top,
now in winter isn't the protective canopy of leaves,
we stand there trembling, what a beautiful world, screwing for peace,
by what comes in, but nobody knows what comes out of it,
if you don't have the past, you don't have to worry about the ridicule,
so always keep a hand's breadth under your keel.

The nature conservation song

it fizzles out on its own.

You are a melody

so new and so neutral.

Like the Swedish forests

for us so cold, so far, so unreachable,

for them so incomprehensible, unrecognized,

for everyone so contrary to the norm,

for many a natural burial.

For the first time, I commissioned a book, "Companero...", but the publisher rejected the book's content, which is unacceptable.
I replied as follows, without being offended:

No problem, I don't think the general public is ready for my book, or even able to make it intellectually understandable as my art, because unfortunately, it seems, they are not yet mature enough for it. That could happen, if the readers' opinion were to change and ostracize me for it, it would certainly be a precautionary measure for me to protect myself from it. It was perhaps too much of a push to become known, but I prefer to proceed in this way by contacting prominent people directly in order to learn from it. Nevertheless, thank you very much, your feedback was valuable to me.

Kind regards,
Yours, Heike Thieme

The common man wants peace and happiness for himself and his family, but people in authority sometimes do not see it or do not want to see it, and do not tolerate dissent.

It is difficult to knock on a closed door, moreover, if the owners are not at home. So it is with people who have all the doors closed in their heads and only one obsession.

I had just had a cherry cola beer
with the father of my children,
and then had my child at his request.
With the agreement that a mother
doesn't need a man to be a father,
and that one day it will be my son
who will steal his father's motorbike
just as he is passing by !

JETZT ODER NIE 1

Imprint

© 2024 Heike Thieme, publishing:
ISBN 978-3-7693-2357-3, BoD · Books on Demand GmbH, In de Tarpen 42, 22848 Norderstedt, bod@bod.de
Print: Libri Plureos GmbH, Friedensallee 273, 22763 Hamburg

Merit does not depend on wealth.

Beauty does not constitute acceptance into the ritual.
Cultural understanding is a universal way of thinking.
Life punishes those who come too late !

Anyone who offers themselves also stands up and leaves.
Anyone who explains themselves looks them in the eyes
and recognizes themselves.
Anyone who recognizes themselves feels sadness,
love and happiness at the same time.
Anyone who does not run away from themselves feels honored
that others admire them.
Anyone who knows how to laugh at themselves
recognizes the irony first in themselves, and then in others.
Anyone who has no shadow in their life looks at it and speaks of love.
Anyone who knows how to handle love, however,
does not waste words on it!
Anyone who has had a long, hard journey in life,
does not have to sell themselves short.
Anyone who works diligently on their destiny will be successful.
Anyone who holds their head proudly high does not have to be
uncomfortable if others would like to see them again as soon as possible.
Anyone who looks forward to friends knows
that life does not give you anything for free.
Anyone who knows how to pay in kind will be recognized.
Anyone who nevertheless admits their own weaknesses will gain a home.

Mon – Ass – Hi! or in short Monarchy!

only means, in view of
the royal misdeeds, internal family atrocities, unfortunate mishaps,
individuals, leaving them alone in the deepest dungeon, leading their fate,
through the darkest alleys, in all dangers,
often simply letting them starve to death..
so much for the ass in the Mon - Ass – Hi!
so now you know why their family was not welcome here, and stood outside
the gates with their arms hanging down, because they deserved i t!
I was so happy, because as a guest there I was the one
who rotted in the deepest dungeon for them!

That's how it's done in the Mon - Ass - Hi :

but the more it becomes known,
how they used you,
how they left you homeless,
how they left you starving,
how they chased you away,
how they laughed at you,
how they raped you three times,
how they never spoke to you,
how they never left you alone,
how they abused you for their fun,
because they knew that one day in your life the moment would come when
the church itself would try the same thing on you, to teach you the Mon -
Ass - Hi , using the simple childish method, giving the little one a slap,
threatening the little one "Don't you dare say anything !"
not giving the little one a job, and despising them !

17

John Kelly speaks out:
"In any case, the presidents is extremely right-wing, in any case he is
authoritarian, he admires dictators, he has said so himself. So he certainly
falls into the general definition of a fascist." Source, New York Times
„Such activity is increasingly out of balance.
He is a threat to the country's security.“

Pirates of today...
the pirates of yesterday,
the profiteers,
the church,
the rockers,
the scoundrels,
the charlatans,
the street vendors -
all just here for a short time
and there again tomorrow!
But what about politics?

Art is survival - is love!
whether "songwriter" or "book author"
illustrative "color maker" in pictures..
True strength comes from within, that's what the stars say
something strong can help the apprentice of life up on a horse
Goblets are drunk when it's foreseeable,
climbing high, hot single sex, autoerotically agile songwriter,
„I love you“ because your works are a blast,
top of the road with "Bier & Kö"
at the gate of truth, the source of knowledge.
tender-stringed like guitars on the bizarre cigar delicacy
so far, have written on 24,000 pages on the bass, tones of thought
laughing, plucking, contradicting way of life wanders through the room
tracking through black and white, the words critical, political, really
dreamlike, harmonious, cheeky!

I HAVE TWO TIGHT GIRLFRIENDS FROM CANADA WHO WENT THROUGH ALL ANIMALISTIC NIGHTMARES –

WHO EXPERIENCED ALL THIS THE SAME !

And because they still held this against her in exile, ... they took her child to do all this to her again, almost in front of my desperate eyes, that she "finally SHUT HER MOUTH!"

A person wants to read, in all those words,
those a friend had written on your skin.
A person wants to guess, when you look for shelter at home,
because he already send you off a house.
A person wants to be like you, going straight and fearless,
because a sick mind doesn't.
A person lingers at your window, because he thinks himself
being the rubbish you'll bring out.
A person fears you from that moment, you bring the rubbish,
when he failed outside and screams for help,
when police will send him to jail guaranteed !

19

Anyone who doesn't want to be on anyone's side,
always leaves the children
growing up in poverty on their own.
If he became a godfather or aunt,
he usually behaves like an outsider,
because the mother is initially made
to understand that they are beautiful and intelligent,
but never enough for her child,
even if she made everyone who thought of her have wet pants,
but never got close to her.

It's like the mayor, who is elected by everyone, and yet he keeps his distance
from the individual citizen his whole life, because that's how he's supposed
to do it, so no one would vouch for your child !

I'll tell you a story about the mother, who, although here and there festivals
were always celebrated without her, because for her that was precisely the
reason she never went where everyone else wanted to go, because she
knows people better.

She also learned to cry as a young child, from laughing.
Showing emotions is more than living Christian charity.
No one should begin to doubt the reality of their soul. Consciousness is a
sensation that also comes from the body. Nobody can define what I am. Our
identity depends on our perceptions. This doesn't need instructions in a
specific concept because the identity does not consist of a constant self.
No magic, no transcendence, no mysticism, no hand of God, no prophetic
knowledge, no law, no transcendent being, the answers to which people
often cannot find in their lives, survived.
We humans are just a walking bundle, undergoing a transformation as time
passes and through the phases of our lives that no one should define in any
individual as just 'despair'.

The solo instrument in addition to the choir is also important. How else does a person want to get to know each other if they do not see themselves as equals to other people and begin to develop independently?

And we must be good but fair, not submissive or stupid, although we ourselves will never be perfect, we humans are like that and at some point in our lives we have applied anti-values or negative skills, the most important thing is that we try to be ourselves to improve and be good. It all depends on how much you believe in yourself to constantly keep them at a distance. Better try to learn from some mistakes we all make. And not to help those who have never felt what love is, because they take their negativity not to thank you, but to harm you for the help you gave.

A sailsman' talents

Get it bet now he had turned all over
and fell out of the hammock from laughter,
he landed on his pampers, special writings for everyone to smile,
has left some farts, while asit on the legs of his new grandma.
I meant songs in his own word flow,
sure like this a good musician is born, early counting the trees,
and counting money bags, some learn to write and speak
before kindergarden, to sing the own texts before running,
my dear Sonboy is such a one.

21

Anyone who wants to make it big in politics reveals how little empathy they have, like a tarantula in the fur of others, who bites when it feels comfortable, PEOPLE is not the intention, will soon be a thing of the past, like the giant, stale glass that they want to invite "friends" to, a little stale, even though the "friends" paid for it themselves, and the work they do will in future be called "PEOPLE" only paying factors, the FACTS from the statements speak for themselves!

Whoever does not begrudge others the water in their glass,
whoever does not refuse the requested sympathy,
whoever gives others their compliments,
whoever does not contradict them,
whoever loves himself,
whoever works hard, should have a break,
whoever is tired as a bear, should have warmth,
whoever sweats like a walrus, should love himself,
whoever lives frugally, should like his surroundings,
whoever has been unhealthy for a long time, should eat whatever he likes,
whoever handles money well, should have known everything about this life!

Souls rise and fall, along the rocks, they feed the fields.
At the bottom of the lake women's game.
Enraged force, these behead the powers.
Waves are like beings, to accompany them to the end and to wander away.
For each other pseudo-truths, animations, thoughts of the rest.

You can not always be in a good mood.
You do not have to always be driven.
There is no such thing as happiness.
But you can use the time, and you can do good,
otherwise the world collapses.
Thoughts glide, true art, to stay on the surface.

First of all, it's just about me. I come first. That's right.
Otherwise, I'm here to chat, nothing more. I'm more of an animal.
So, what does the sect want here? I celebrate myself, I don't need drugs.
So, what do I mean to you? I see the fraudsters, businessmen, who rip off
their clientele.
So, am I supposed to play slave for them, and take part in the mess?
I'm always alone. So why boast to me, that I 'd buy all their Crêpe 5 oeufs?
I'm only loyal to myself. So nobody is like me,
if you want to imitate me, you go home alone.
I'm just finding myself right now. So that's exactly what matters.
I won't have to socialize here,because I've been that way all my life anyway.

Setting boundaries is very easy,

first you say, girl, what do you think your mother will say

about you walking around the street at night,

and wanting to sit on strangers' couches?

second you say, girl, that you have family here in town,

no, that's not right, ask your mother first,

where she comes from!

third you say, girl,

it's normal that I don't turn around for people,

am not the personification of information,

who wants to know all that, it's none of my business,

don't have to invite people for coffee,

so read my novels,

or better take care of your dog!

The princess lives in the belief that she is very close to her brother, as if she knew for her entire life whether he was angry about something.

The woman from the office took advantage of the night
Waiting to see when everyone will be unemployed
to have eyes, look up into them,
the informer who opens his mouth,
to follow his finger and feel validated,
which pregnant woman he is pointing at.

The man employed by the office,
only works in the chicken snack bar but still,
who is considered a citizen,
but who feels outcast at night, like a vampire,
and hides the fact that he likes to play the pharmacist to everyone.

The citizen, who feels misunderstood,
is insulted because everyone thought
that his best friend had taken his own life because of him.
They immediately accuse him of being a false person
who wishes death on others.
They all curse him until their eyes almost pop out
and they lose their voice.

Animal cycle
Natural cycle
Life cycle
Climate cycle
Disturbed natural course...
is perhaps the same as ignoring it, we humans belong to these cycles,
even our bodies function in circles !

it is certainly the person who is most harmed,
whose inner balance is disturbed, by a mental crisis for example,
whoever falls out of the concept of cycles, not infrequently commits suicide,
so a humanly endangered species, from a purely technical point of view,
because THAT DOES NOT MIND PEOPLE within a SOCIETY EVEN !

HUMAN BEINGS PUT THEMSELVES IN DANGER !

All mismanagement is now being passed on massively to the insured and
society because the federal government is bankrupt,
leaving out the prestigious private insurers,
they are being asked whether they themselves would be willing,
only voluntarily, to make a financial contribution to save the hospitals?

Politicians ask...: "Hey, guys, it can't be that it's always the same people who
get involved. It would be really nice if the private companies got involved
too!"

The current state of the medical sector is sick, the drug supply bottlenecks,
the Health Care Strengthening Act, a litany of humility, appeal on CD,
patients with health insurance pay double!

Regarding the Health Minister's Paypal link:
all private providers such as DEBEKA, like BARMENIA,
like SIGNAL IDUNA, like HALLESCHE, like HANSE MERKUR......
have left the Whatsapp group !

If everyone believes they would have the right about the normal rules
of living together to put away, who exercise VIOLENCE on women,
also about their CHILDREN, EXCLUDE mothers professionally,
until the DISCRIMINATION occurs here really nice IN-NORTH,
defy all LAWS, like the businessmen, like the church, like politicians
like the rockers, like the scoundrels, like the charlatans, like the hawkers,
then they will ALL end up LEAVE EMPTY ONE DAY !

The south slaughters women, as if men had been taught,
trained, almost fluently, to hate women from the ground up.

The north extends the farce by allowing arbitrary laws from the Weimar era
to prevail freshly, piously, happily, freely, making them speechless,
depriving women of any chance in any respect.

These two systems mesh with each other, work flawlessly and callously,
imposing on women multiple suffering in the violation of the human rights,
in the lewdness of every encounter, confronting them up to 100,000 times
with the fact that women have no say in Germany.

But at some point the beard is gone,
and she wears her hair with pride,
she sued EVERYONE, from the autobiography onwards,
until no boy or girl can touch it,
because she tells everyone to their face,
and in a seemingly wise way, they recognize their stupidity,
and drunkards recognize their incompetence,
and sick encounters lose friends,
and fraudsters hold the woman up as a graduate!

So don't anyone tell me on the street,
stopping me, that I just have to describe briefly,
without buying any books or investing in the art of living,
the 100,000 cases of discrimination I have experienced in my life!

To be the friend of man
to act automatically
The question is how ?

The marriage market
a vague promise
awareness excluded

The object of a thing
puffs up, takes off
in the distance

Where seen as a sign
don't go for it
was like this before

At the finish the rain pours
at the summit rift
no way down

Where is the journey going ?
Reason kept
against or for ?

The strong being
Presence in use
shakes the story

30

The princess lives in the belief that she is very close to her brother, as if she
knew for her entire life whether he was angry about something ?
What she was angry about ? What felt damn close to her ?

The woman from the office took advantage of the night
Waiting to see when everyone will be unemployed
to have eyes, look up into them,
the informer who opens his mouth,
to follow his finger and feel validated,
which pregnant woman he is pointing at.

The man employed by the office,
only works in the chicken snack bar but still,
who is considered a citizen,
but who feels outcast at night, like a vampire,
and hides the fact that he likes to play the pharmacist to everyone.

The citizen, who feels misunderstood,
is insulted because everyone thought
that his best friend had taken his own life because of him.
They immediately accuse him of being a false person
who wishes death on others.
They all curse him until their eyes almost pop out and they lose their voice.

I am the bearer of the message! I am the rapist of evil!
I am the singing five-faced people from SCHLESWIG!
I am the spiritual RUNWAY for the PHILOSOPHICAL AIRSHIPS
of the FUTURE! I am a warning and a REMINDER!

I see that it is no longer read ! As a writer, that is very unfortunate!
I've been watching for 40 years how the brains of all province shrinking,
the young people cover them with extra-large black moped helmets,
the old people later show it off with covered lawnmower mopeds
that they use for shopping, like the MAYA THE BEE HANDBAG!

Without a future - no future
a little tree on the left, a little tree on the right,
and you still dare to dream, standing in front of the trees,
and looking up to the top,
now in winter isn't the protective canopy of leaves,
we stand there trembling, what a beautiful world, screwing for peace,
by what comes in, but nobody knows what comes out of it,
if you don't have the past, you don't have to worry about the ridicule,
so always keep a hand's breadth under your keel.

The nature conservation song, it fizzles out on its own.
You are a melody so new and so neutral. Like the Swedish forests
for us so cold, so far, so unreachable,
for them so incomprehensible, unrecognized,
for everyone so contrary to the norm,
for many a natural burial.

I am the bearer of the message.
I am the rapist of evil.
I am the singing five-faced figure from Schleswig.
I am the spiritual runway
for the philosophical airships of the future.
I am the admonisher and the reminder !

Oh, i know who has the entrance to work out here.
This is the hypocrat for church,
this is the liar from each religious sect,
this is the wannabe mom of anything, and the womb is winning,
the religion wants to be the winner, the lie and liar,
HE and SHE works it out.
Useful educated empathic people are even not enough for a together walk,
the adress is easy forgotten, the birthdate is a useful toy,
to give the own child what it gets, and you stand outside of the window,
while she is throwing a bite down for you dog !

Vote is kinda splitted in
wether "Prosit Alcohol !" or otherwise "Welcome Pain !"
the one who is untalented, the other one is unsympathically,
people would say to both, better none of them...
is like sugar or salt, both too much, is like ignorance to facts,
is like blaming the folks, who actually have to do the work in comparison,
like pushing the blackrock, like loosing political trust, like shrinking brains,
I'm out of this system, I am old, is like pains in the Ass !

Hello, my lovelies, I unfortunately have to stay in the room alone because of
the open wound. I'm just making the best of it.

My friends always tell me, no matter what happens, we know that we will
win the last battle, taking advantage of the peace and quiet, even if it hurts,
it's always an opportunity to know what you're willing to give up!

My left knee is infected around the knee and it hurts like hell. Stay loyal to
me, even if I can't get in touch for a while.

If the pain breaks down the walls, let yourself be warmed up with soft water,
I'd like to hold your hand tightly, then we can drink, booze and party again
afterwards!

My lovelies, I'm not feeling so well at the moment. I'm taking a break first.
My surroundings I have a bit of a fever and have to go to the hospital
tomorrow. What crap....

I spray it on every wall, the country needs new men, today we don't agree
with what's going on, we grin now, we cut off our braids because we've
reached that age ! We have science on our side, but we all lack the
soundtrack to say what it's about, without groove there's no move, only with
art can you change the world ! I'll give you one good reason why I'm
committed to forests, we're inside, get back on your feet, the bark beetles do
better lobbying work!

I see too in the power hungry leader one, who...
never has competence,
not socially,
not communicative,
not scientific futurally,
not stabilizing a country, like psychotherapist would call it he is missing too
much of cognitive approach to language teaching that emphasizes
interaction as both the means That is what the study says !!!

Anyone who is as wrong as the man,
whose ability to be a partner as a rapist is ZERO,
who doesn't even send one of them out to lay the eggs in a relationship,
as we have seen here,
would simply be canned in jars with the cucumbers in the autumn !

Get up for your future ! Meant stand on long legs.
Fall in love and Go for it ! Meant leave the fight.
Find the path to go, as all do.

My hearth is warmth. My tattoo is no competition. My dart is my vader.
My friend came from wandering, which path did You come from ?

THE EXPERT ADVICE... in the event that
What does a man do who is not that tall when he has to pee,
and yet believes in his power, in his delusions of grandeur,
to destroy an entire human world,
does he then enlist the help of his friends
who lift him up especially, and hold his little dick?

I advise every now and then,
to litter the local newspaper with articles saying
that a pasha himself is only suitable for porn,
but not for standing up pissing, d certainly not in politics!
What has the man... DONE WRONG?

I know him in three voices, the fatherly voice cried out in concern, in a high female voice!

I know him as a perpetrator, the bungler booms out, who is afraid for his own balls!

I know him as a misunderstood person, who made puppets dance in his youth, today a rather supposed gay man!

Is he a father, does no one hear it? Is he the one who assaults women?
Is he without any good figure? Is he the one who is noticed by everyone?

THE HOLYWOOD KISS more false than its promise.
I will never, ever stand up and offer myself naked to those
whose skin is grey and their eyes are dull,
their smiles are frozen and their feet are rough,
towards the sucking smile,
whose fetish is only whining and panting,
who have searched for each other all their lives
and never found each other,
who have never given their love to a woman,
and pretended to be whoever they wanted,
who drink liquor when they are unwell,
who stink of garlic when they have the flu,
who drink lemons dry and inhale eucalyptus,
who look like fish even in the water,
who may be good swimmers, but they will never be heroes!

LOVE in the COLD WAR is not LOVE - no TIME for it
whoever knows himself - knows it ENOUGH,
or he or she becomes a rabbit in the frying pan,
without ever being allowed to have the awareness of it !

A young graduate trainee
has no educational knowledge,
has not yet given birth to a child,
has not yet worked for free,
maybe has been involved in something here and there,
has not understood simplicity,
has no routine in working life,
has not put theory into practice,
has hardly any idea of human crises,
because she has not worked on herself,
has not practiced partnerships,
is ignorant of the real, unprivileged working life,
has only just begun to look around in her young life,
never knows the place here, the across,
no salto mortale, from here to there,
and not the whole outside,
the middle, the forward backwards among people,
made herself rare and unattainable,
only picking out the best bits in passing,
making a name for herself with the knowledge of others,
but still wants to be the one to claim
to know everything, to know the truth,
to give unsolicited advice to deny others' competence,
how else would she one day gain respect?

People, the young people today don't want to work anymore,
they're called students now, with a privileged background,
that is, without any knowledge, but sometimes we meet,
and maybe one twin will talk to another, and both realize that
people pounce on anything that's offered for free for advertising purposes,
to steer them in their tracks, and to suck their blood,
they have the same knowledge of human nature,
but only one of those privileged ones
can pick out the best bits, right?

We live in such an idyllic place, don't we?
The neighbor is always far away from us.
The German agrees. We live Swedish crispbread.
We use half a pound of butter for it.
We thank the meadow, the hill, the stupid sheep,
and lie on our bikes on paths, to push pedestrians away.
We extract oil from the North Sea, so it finances a village,
and the Wadden Sea, that used to be,
now we extract oil fresh from the water.
Oh, yes, we are very fond of Sweden, we always talk about it,
it's quite normal, with the only mackerel in our pots!

Toxic amnesia.

This is another way to describe gaslighting. A toxic person deliberately tells
you that your reality isn't real. When it is very real. They don't want to be
accountable, so they deny your memory.

You are NOT crazy

So what, you put him to Catmountain,
then leave him with his family
then see him with his friends
drive home to Christmas in a car,
it might be Upsala, also might be Uttica,
the same all over again,
they fight in that ride home,
and the one calls the other a demon,
when i think about them all,
then see them all drown
in a romantic drive through snow and ice.
But ask myself, thinking about these chicks,
is there anyone worth it in that car,
or ain't - and i know the answer.

A sailsman and nice pirate died 3 years ago, he wrote some little books at the end and partied with everyone from his pirate isle, until the end, yes, but you see, if he is just 3 years gone, he is still aware as if he never had left !!! hahaha i see he didn't still block or unfollow me !!!

donald johnson
@EcuadorDon

Get it bet now he had turned all over and fell out of the hammock from laughter, it is like that if i love someone i do not let him fall, we can be aware that he was reborn on this dreamy isle and wups now he is climbing around on his first sail boat, so he landed on his pampers.

And writing his own special writings for everyone to smile, no first he has to go to school, maybe he is watching us in winter all asit around the christmas tree, and laughing about that bullshit, no he is no ugly person, i am talking about emotion and humor, maybe his ass has left some farts, while asit on the legs of his new grandma. I meant songs in his own word flow, sure like this a good musician is born, some learn early counting the trees, and money bags, some learn to write and speak before kindergarden, some learn to sing the own texts before running, my dear Sonboy was such a one. I talked much with him, he knew more about computers before maths, yes, talking was good in the pauses, when he came to me, mostly reading fairy, and philosophy with kids stoff, he just went to school because we wanted him to, and the math he just accepted, because i had explained him math for beginners with warmth. But nowadays teachers are misanthropists. The grade learning of factories i know now what my son meant with that, all that he learned to know the skills, and believe how to do things came from the love of his mother, that the very opposite is meant, what you bring home from school was just bully. I really do know now why my son years long stepped from one cold to another, and from one migraine to the next, science told us, migraine has its roots from mature beings who play the role as brainwashers, that this poor pupils from today are all underwised how to beat the weaker, to press the other down, to be hated by their teachers.

Learn the bully some as good as it gets, until one suicides.
This is the usual character of kids from the age and mental standard of
kindergarden, and nothing changes in schools to a higher level, even not a
tip of the pedagoge ideas, ok that was all for today, i am not willing to fall
behind this lowest level.

LET THIS FORGET AND LOOK FORWARD ! What an in between !
A work of art made by hands, what is really great about the wanted, is her
big mouth, and the bruises, but where is the mark of her love, which only
went downhill, if she only takes a break from sex with everyone now and
then? I am doing all within silence.

In this country they are dying like flies.
We are talking about people in care, while also the nurses,
who are mentally broken, those who are abandoned by burnout,
those who are retired early, even those who are traumatized, should,
according to the church, NEVER AGAIN be allowed to return to normal
social work and have a chance of retirement.
You can have learned ten professions, written 127 books in 10 years,
be unmatched in terms of language Vice Versa,
always been straightforward and successfully raised alone,
but if you lose your job and are left with no prospects, because it is simply
intended that way for no reason that their faces become greyer and greyer
and they only meet you as passers-by, then even after ten years you will still
hear in your neighbourhood how you are compared to the plague because
you are unemployed, and everything is shared, including your offers and
gifts, but only from the street, and it should stay that way!
Abroad, it is only talked about in the evening illustrious scene,
where gays die in large numbers from AIDS. But here in Germany,
as described above, a society is once again being destroyed by excessive
demands and bullying, because of a society that is becoming colder !!!!!

I know that feeling.
But i am 60 now, knowing how to handle it.

The Love in your eyes proves, that the envy and egoistic ones,
do not want the ability you have. Once you will travel in dreams
and wonder how many times that you changed the directions in life,
how many professions you learned,
and studied working life, this is the only thing to learn,
and nobody else is interested in you,
but You my heart, that i tell you that i love you,
and embrace you, to make your way,
and give you blessings from my heart,
the house of life is so small, that your big house needs to arrange,
to still find a place in that, ...

HAPPY BIRTHDAY DEAR GOOD FELLOW !

Our political chamgagne builds a fruity chuicy mixture,
we have those who do not trust in this, but chose the same lame duck,

we have those who prove how … a government that exists on paper,
show how to overthrow without shame,

we have those who pretend in church, and say clear the fact,
threaten the voter right at the kitchen table, press into their thought system,
warn not to heat in winter, and ... build a huge confusion !
So here we are dealing with a judgmental six! Deviant behavior not borne of
decency and integrity, but... Because of stupidity and attempted deception !
The drippy Air once was the Boomer Age Party ! live fast die young,
now noooo, best ager nowadays lie in the sun !

The funny thing is,
when you don't let people disrespect you,
they start calling you difficult.
I know, people hate also,
when you just have a question,
then explode for nothing,
people hate also,
when you ask for a saver way to drive a car,
because it frightens you,
people also hate, when you and the kids are aware,
that family is just "a pretend to be"
... but then i just give them the advice,
to read all my novels,
and be good to the dog !

43

He who likes to play God,
thought his twin was different, and different is a competitor,
because his father likes him more, sibling envy blossoms,
has its origins in myths, the invasion of negative feelings,
goes all the way to the top of the mountain,
there his will dwells in bad blood, to make the exchange,
to step into his brother's shoes, to first destroy what annoys him,
then take on the role of the beloved, not one who thought himself at the top,
although it is known that their shameful deed does not expire,
and inadvertently comes to light!

UNCLE FRITZ'S WRONG JOKE ! If I were a woman now,
who had never counted her butterflies,
who had never turned around unexpectedly,
who had never remembered which song came to mind
when he played the part for her outside,
who had never jumped from one side of the road to the other to run right
into the arms of the goat, and had never said a word about the trans man
next to her freaking out with anger because she didn't go to church with him,
but only noticed that in this case was the wrong decision to cut off his dick!
If I met myself as such a boring cow, outside on the park bench,
I would make sure to leave the city as quickly as possible !

A beautiful woman asks me on the bench "Are you up for it?"
while a goat is standing behind our bench scolding us both,
I say "No, he's not up for it either!" both sit in silence in the void,
then a stranger with white hair comes,
I say "Look, there's Grandma coming!" still an awkward silence,
the beautiful woman calls out to the passerby at the same time
"Can I join you?" and she's gone, leaving the city.
I'm not stopping here for a quick snack, whose great love dumped her
for the show, because the fun is no longer so fruitful at some point,
I'm not the bargain on the park bench, to let off steam, because the woman
tolerated me taking the discarded love's dachshund out for a walk!

HELLO, I'm not mad at you ! I say HELLO to you, that sounds like a
MOIN-MOIN here, and is meant as if I were stroking your long, white
beard, right behind me walks my little GRANDMA, who is dressed in her
knitted sweater, and she only likes to walk behind me in the dark, so as my
GRANDMA'S PROTECTOR, and it's always like that SHE LOVES YOU !

When a punk explained love to me,
he had left me at the highest moment, then I wanted to die,
but the self-love in me, hit me like a hiccup, that I laughed at myself,
I looked myself in the eyes, I knew I would be scared now
then in three days I would be dead on the rails,
I looked at myself for a long, warm time
and then laughed for days, ten hours a day,
then you just think about O - - - - and just have him,
'Cause every song I sang to trees. I laughed again, and I had to watch
my feet, but it feels really good to have this inner protector like self-love!

Isn't it funny ??? when the sexiest thing in the morning
wakes up and your good dear fellow stands aside telling .....
"Man, you look like a turnshoe, and even like that you smell !"
just fine, i say then, knowing, that i have finally to get up,
or the coffee gets cold .....
- HEIKE THIEME - YLVA -
yes, but i gave her to answer that it is tolerated like that,
because anyway it is best to get up no chance, than hang on the floor
till aftermidday, sounds like a staubsauger from grandma,
and is just the provocation never to give up,
what all had to be done today, more with an insult,
but to do what had to be, what is important
and not to do, what you really like to do.

When authoritive sinners try to express their ambitions, it minimizes, the bear in bed, the beer in head, the mighty friend in holiday, the meat on plate, the file how to registrate, the warmest pullover for winter, the authoritive advices for poorness, the loss of carrier in all levels, the unemployed mass, the drunken Christmas 2024 !

Carpenter or Spanish gigolo!
Queens always get jealous,
they crave love that they don't feel,
they work for their lack of love, after all,
and that brings in money,
but for that they would steal every neighbor's guy once,
just to look away from their escapades,
but the walls around her are thick,
the men who turn her down, unless they are taken,
and she lets a discord be blessed for herself,
just to get what she wants,
that's quite normal, the others are open-minded,
so if her money wins, she'll just be jealous
Young, virile, enjoying wildness because it can be bought,
love is always about money.
All this open-mindedness is pointless !!

When the worst insult so, it is to publicly present
your favourite stinking turnshoe, why then not admit,
if You would be just invited by the FUCK FINGER ??

TRY THIS OUT!!!
Everyone always wants to be a Viking!
They believe it is because they love the old days so much
that they fall into the stupidity of showing empathy for people,
while diving into the depths of the ocean for everyone
to dig up all their suffering.

As if the wise man was a one-eyed mane lion, whose love for people,
spread across his whole face in a smile, who takes them all home,
and shows everyone the right way, offers the newly rich a parking deck,
the poor the affection that everyone deserves.

But I still can't decide today, or I think it is unnecessary to
decide to live for the rich or the poor version, and to feel elevated !

Who would but once in their life,
have to admit that he has roof damage,
in the most hostile interior of the heart, misanthrope,
and as humorless as a spree cucumber in a preserving jar?

Oh, people, why not agree to a year
of voluntary work with the police?
Then spend a year as a mandatory temporary worker,
basically a year as a crime scene corpse.

Oh, people, why not agree to a year of voluntary work
with a church organization?
Then use it as a year of commitment,
for a clientele that is only marginally looked at,
fed, managed and washed for reasons of economy.

Oh people, why not agree in a voluntary year
in the Bundeswehr?
Then spend a year earning quite well as an intern,
better than in the social sector,
and being seen as more social
than social workers in the church !

Heike Thieme

Gezeitenwandel - im Zauber erhaben

Donald 'Amigo Don' Johnson
Ecuador John – The Treasure Hunter !

We thought would be good with some kind of Twitter manifestation.
This days our nice pirate friend and adventurer has passed.
This time I am so speechless,
maybe You will find the right words to our friend.

I join in. The everytime joy reading Donald 'Amigo Don' Johnsons tweets
and comments brought smiles and laughs, always giving of himself to make
a brighter day. And reading that little rant of
HandyDandyBrandyGubbaRumCoffee was like a little happy spell !

like he found to his own hammock over the paradise ocean...
like mummy does hold him finally back in her arms...
like all the friends still keep on his golden words...
like none would ever forget
how to fight through the everyday
when see what he as pirate has done...
like he would crumble in the white sand as Turtle egg
and shall soon to be seen again...
like we all miss his friendly voice, because he was so fatherly...
like who ever knows when to meet such an adventurer again...
like we let him go, but once soon will reach him in our best dreams...

Blessings from us all

Education is not the learning of facts,
but the training of the mind to think. - Albert Einstein -

The war is not meant to be won,
it is meant to be continous. - George Orwell -

Those who cannot change their minds, cannot change anything.
- George Bernard Shaw -

You will always regret, what you did not do, rather than what you did.
I say, if you lost the chance to feel sorry, for what you did,
you lost the chance to live in truth, for that day you will struggle,
you lost the chance to recieve help,
for the case that you never learned.. to recieve or to give !
Beautiful that smile in you... if it wouldn't be that laughable,
will always be stuck behind you, in that distance inside a car,
you will never become mature, but for your friends..
you will knick out of their ways, when they would definitely need you.

Two guys live in puberty, stuck together not look at you,
higher than you on top of a horse,
not to be touched by the ground, the people walk on,
shy to greet, run away on horses feet, coward like a mom's good son,
maybe wanna be to become heroes, but will never be,
because in a danger situation, the bemome two creeps.

Once loaded, always loaded, in comparison to Bin Laden,
a guy who was raised among brutal people,
no lie, also went through boot camps, was forced upon him,
pulled through once on his father's leash,
did not escape a difficult childhood,
but spent his whole life trying to make money, the inferiority complex
he had already acquired as a small boy, with power over people,
with being seen as a moneybag, but finally to be noticed ONCE in his life !

The rich guy, told everyone, what's given is given,
"It's all YOUR own fault that you didn't have a rich father to pass on!"
now he makes the decision, because money is power,
and dreams of doing business with the Martians,
with his planetary atmospheric vacuum cleaner,
with x - ONE TIME sucking away all these useless bits and bites,
and ensuring CLEANLINESS, and it will one day
be a best seller on EARTH, because being rich has to be really rich !

I was against it when I was 18
model career decided, because then it just said
"Kitchen" - "Marriage" - "Fatherland"
my answer "Resistance!" after that,
my planned path was pretty bumpy because of my family,
I didn't let myself be marketed,
so their hatred of the family increased !

Diversity ... the top models are looking for advertising,
even among the less % looking.
Positivity ... the top models are looking for wannabees,
also to upgrade shrunken brains.
Personality ... the top models are looking for talent,
even among the less talented.
... that's all, I have nothing more to contribute, and goodbye!

The one ABOVE EVERYTHING ever existed
unmatched of yourself BELOVED, lump of human,
according to the DIY kit provided with a real eye,
the lump two extra expensive breasts,
the comedy again, the eye that is cast upon them,
the wig of her curls with the mangle also turned,
and for improvement injected with the insemination syringe Botox,
Eyebrows in the shape of an Ikea key, Anyone can do that
MAKE SOMETHING OUT OF HIS TYPE !

Who would be interested in a party
refuses to loosen the brakes until all industry throws in the towel?
Who would be interested in a babyface who plays the role of destroyer
himself, the route is calculated,
whose future doom-mongering of politics and anti-democratic attitude
would be better, one should advise, not to have children in it,
who is so stupid as to do that?
at a police checkpoint "Yes, Sergeant, I'm completely crazy, but only at
work level, keep going! and I've also abolished all traffic lights!"
In these matters too, a clear 0:0 in terms of knowledge gain!
If 10,000 citizens listening to this debacle actually feel extremely
uncomfortable with what is being addressed,
Wow - that means double-digit interest..

The old-fashioned marital form,
means to them that the woman stays at home cooking,
the dark-haired children should not go to kindergarten,
the constellation also says: "It's father." "It's mother." and "It's wife." -
so for all brothel visitors, as a rule, the "second wife" is meant by that!
Statistically: "Every fourth man is such a customer!" so out of 100 it's 25%
then, dear housewife, ".... t
he little housework takes its own place, says my husband !"

The miner goes to work the night shift,
to the woman, it's the lover's turn.
All you need to 'cheat' is a migraine,
the other 'version' promises 'salvation'.
Agreeing who belongs in her boat,
puts the lady of the house in distress.
The future of wealth, the lust for the flesh,
everyone is standing still, she remains frustrated.
The whole thing is laughable: "Hats off!"
Sappo has succeeded in her race to ridicule.

Tonight in the dream two baby horses came from above, a white horse and a black young horse, both of which had kissed me from above on the forehead for a long time, as often as they could. I also had the other dream when I visited some elderly people in an old pub in Schleswig in the evening, sat at their table and read to them from my three secret books, as if these books were filled with ancient wisdom, so that I knew in the dream, they said, that I had never needed to ask a doctor for help in my life ! That's why I've always said that I'm neither neurotic nor sick, the many dreams I have always tell of the real world that is connected to me.

I know my Scoliosis is a fact, and sure i make it with gymnastic to strenghten me, so if pains returned, that i find big help in Chakra meditation to minimize the pains, and then start to train the muscles, that worked immediately healing strong, and i had not had pains since years now, to keep my ears clean i ususally pump warm water inside to make them free of small parts, i have no panic with this. That with the eyes is sure, so i will go and test it, my eyes find good help to wear online or with TV a blue-light-eye glas, that calmed the eyes much, to dream even better, those glasses with yellow eyeglas are the better one option. The best of all is my psyche is the best condition ever !!! and that is what i thank for guaranteed and greatfully, and for the feet and knees and against pains i usually wear military lady boots above the ankles, those stabilize my ankles and let me walk painfree, and as much as i want may go on wanderings with my dog. I am no more afraid of tics, too, because one time i heard about the scientific newcoming medicine from January next year to vaccination against borelliosis for a file of 30 bucks, and second since i found out to give my labrador each day a small spoon by giving black cumin oil, the right B vitamins, or sometimes tea tree oil on the fur, we didn't bring any more ticks home this year.

So it is just needed to be good informated how to treat yourself and your fellows well, and all functions well !!!

A friend gets this words from me - For me, you are the kind of person I would describe as a horse expert. You always had the right instinct for women who are, believe it or not, good for nothing other than sausages, and you tell them straight to their faces what you want because they know how to deal with their own and other people's truths. From my point of view, the only real solution is to try to live with other people, to live with the truth, and to know people and horses well. How else is it supposed to work?

Yes, the brave mother suffered labor pains. She admits it hurt.
What opened her eyes afterwards. No other people far and wide.
There isn't so much to see. No Lion King, she is not the Lion's Bride.
No singing up to the rock, no sunset named after them.
Just the screaming of all the hyenas.
She puts the situation in order like a soldier,
fills her entire life into a comic, inside you can see colors,
and trees, grass and only that, but she hasn't met any people since.
Only a few henchmen, they sneak up to the baby's bed and steal it.

Gropers portray themselves as victims, the crowd is getting their coffee
they are in a public jam, the crowd is probably short of breath
they just step on women's legs,
they're better off looking past the women's gazes,
they talk rubbish, their ears are deaf, the women are about to throw up
the moaning gropers, also retire, well paid by the way!
Gropers who get older are seen like an old sick man look, it also somehow
feels like a personal transgression, isn't it, really bad, huh?

After years, my first used laptop broke down, now I've found a second one with Windows 7 on eBay, I just have to restart it again, but the data is all well looked after, nothing is lost, that's what happens when you see your notebook slide off your pillow a little, where it then hugs your coffee cup and the thing is gone, and I thought that since I have a lap-rador that has lived with me for 13 years and is indestructible, the laptop would last forever without any problems, but it happens as it comes, damn technology!

Have you heard that widely spread degitalizing of schools in Denmark brought the fact, that none of the kids will learn anything out of books anymore ? Sothat they started the way back to minimize that development and bring back book into schools ? It is very important as i always say to all kids. It is better to act with your imagination and creative thinking, consuming pre-chewed food has not stimulated a young brain to maturity.

The FEYNMAN technique of learning:
STEP 1 - Pick and study a topic

STEP 2 - Explain the topic to someone, like a child, who is unfamiliar with the topic

STEP 3 - Identify any gaps in your understanding

STEP 4 - Review and Simplify!

Roman Empire
CONFLICTS ARE NOT RESOLVED BY TOSKING A COIN
The RECOGNITION EFFECT IS IN HISTORY!

Who would fall for that?
The USA is at its last moment,
a coin toss away knowing that its empire could fall,
certain that its functioning system can collapse in a minute,
certainly every life there has an end,
but so does a 400-year-old democracy.
If these people were to decide TODAY
to close their fate as a civilization with a slam
like a book and end it, then they would have chosen the
FASTEST WAY, the coin would fall and while it was still flying,
they would have determined totalitarianism, and they know that
this Roman Empire would be irreparable in one of their last generations!

COLD LOVE !
A LOVE BOUND IN A COLD WAR....

The idea we all lived on an island, is overdue...
your little sweeties with freckles on her face like a shot in the oven,
the eyes end up tiny and fall on the street in front of me,
and no one has ever picked them up, a love farce has gotten lost,
and never rises from the grave again,
and who will please you, get the toilet paper on that day,
roll your joint in the morning, warm the Senorina's bed,
make the world more beautiful from the first date,
which is no longer a WORLD in itself?

Vacation and No Cost ! Fantastic scenery!
Birds are singing, the house has been hijacked,
the sneakers are green, the roof beams are brown,
white everywhere, the cozy shirt, fresh from the bedsheet,
white curtains everywhere, the neighbor invites us in,
we bring him wine, just like that on the island,
we are all alone, just took a wrong turn,
on the wrong island, and the house is newly occupied,
vacation for nothing, and at no cost,
the neighbor invites us in, and the rooms are cleaned, as befits.
Of course "Alma" and "Pablo" will leave it clean.

I love my grazy girlfriend !
An old dog doesn't learn old tricks anymore.
We just got to know each other.
It felt like that three years ago.
We argued with old acquaintances.
She's standing in front of me on the beach at night.
She was the most beautiful sight of the day.
She had the hottest ass.
She's suited to the hottest doggy style.

She's checking it out, as his gaze deduces.
Outside in the dark afterwards, is like before as a couple in old age,
the joint of youth, where everything happens, seriously maybe the time of
the partnership is over, like a phase of life, and in old age have no stress.

Mademoiselle, … is perfectly fine cheats a little with her colleague,
goes on holiday with her friend, mistaken about the address,
felt comfortable in the stranger's house, passed on the holidaymakers,
is a good cleaner with him, he leaves everything immaculately clean,
the Mademoiselle, meanwhile, is melancholy,
her life is not so perfect after all, but sees the paying guests in exchange
with her and calls out, "Everything is clean, dear guests, everything is
perfect, bye, welcome to my island !" and sneaks out to collect her friend.

It is less to gain as sacrifice,
than to win, because you mastered all contests in your life !
They say, in the morning when you get up...
"She doesn't like me" we sleep together, but she doesn't like me,
it's completely fine, nobody likes me anyway, I hardly like myself,
but I like everyone else even less than myself,
maybe that's the case with her too,
maybe she likes me a little after all?

Why is holding me a single, horny mother for ennobled,
just because she's bored standing right in front of me,
wobbling on her high heels, touching me alone,
assigned me to work, thinks I'm the sun but prevents me
in her plush and jacket, the chic black one,
staring at me horny, at this, my workplace
to DO my WORK?

What prevents women from publishing old stories,
all those from their phases of life?
Why are they afraid to take their hobby organic farm,
where they grew up with the piglets, for granted?
What do they avoid admitting that a fine little nose is intended to prevent
how many things they steal from others,
their secrets, their stories, their souls,
whatever was useful, to pursue a career?

Who is sucking you dry.
Standing there again in a checkerboard coat signals,
daughter needs to get married. Daughter is already dreaming …
wetly in the morning. Daughter just needs one... the one with muscles,
the one who is young and naive enough,
the one who is submissive and helpful,
the one who has a mother-in-law's dream.
Now it's time to match up, says mom.

How does Miss Wannabe ask herself,
is there going to be a future,
if everyone is only thinking about being healthy,
if they go easy on their knees and go hiking,
if they go easy on their eyes and write,
if they look after dogs, cats, horses and children,
and know something about caring for the elderly,
if they always already know everything from experience,
if they have a sense of humor and laugh at nonsense,
if they read between the lines,
if they are cautious,
if they don't confuse stupid nonsense,
if they smile at hypocritical amateur therapists,
if they don't reveal knowledge when requested,
because they have learned the knowledge that only those who find it out for
themselves will know something about this, their life!

RAVEN CHILDREN !!
Isn't it always obvious how for bunglers
the PROSPECT of enrichment builds up such internal pressure
that they could lose in it, so it is usually also innate, passed on from parents,
such complicity above all else, even in the case of financial failure,
and inappropriate WEALTH, that RAVEN CHILDREN also
drive away a SIBLING, because it has a HEART !

Mother testified to me that that is quite normal, as they say,
of a kind of "LIFE SUPPORT", which meant
collective beatings, threats, bullying,
expulsion, rejection, locking away,
initiating dangerous situations, child removal,
oh, simply EVERYTHING that was loving and GOOD....
because it was only the BEST for me, teaching me through parental care
how one would then crawl up to them in humility, respect and consent,
as the PROPHECY wanted, to teach me decency and MARRIAGE!

Halloween here is not really modern, we had today reformations day in the
north a new holiday, then they will soon walk out with the kids at night for a
lantern walk in town on my birthday the 11th november. I would say here in
the north it is province, the south Kiel, north Flensburg, but all between is
kinda country side, that i read in newspaper that youngsters in north only in
Flensburg city have 75 % success with highschool degrades, with
highschool i meant the end of school, not the successful study, but in Kiel
55%, in the country side is about 30%, and in poor Schleswig and around
only 25%, so i do live in the most stupid area here around, that even more
and more young women end with a complete study, and lesser men, who
break up early.; it is only that here in town we have the usual street lanterns,
but a few kilometers from here live more cows than humans, and the nights
are dark outside. If men will loose the step into carrier, then not find the
trick to balance their live early, and study disciplined, then many more men
will loose the chance to enfold their talents in future.

Touching a book by a show host
or letting an ageing show host grope you...?
I've always been into art, but not on top of the stage like him.
At this point I wouldn't touch either even if it was written in GPT
and empty as a bean pod with a pair of pliers !

Find yourself after birth
your child first in zombie land,
you seem to have all this around you,
to embody, regardless of
that you long for peace,
the man rushes off like a prince,
the candles light up to keep the Jehovahs out,
the pantomime becomes an illusion,
the sects rush by like a tsunami,
the caretakers find themselves hanged on top,
the friends can't get up,
the cows themselves say "No comment" to everything,
the journey into the mountains, you just want to get out,
the waters all seem dirty,
the dogs only have lice hidden in their fur,
the lives of soldiers well consider the same,
the authorities monitor Mrs. Mother like a leper,
the mothers chase after you with suggestions for improvement,
the box of wine empties quickly and silently with loyal people,
the wine sellers don't give you any more wine,

.... simply because she say,
"You better not drink so much alcohol, that wouldn't be good !"
WHY SO SERIOUS? THAT WAY OUT!!
THAT WAS MY VERY INDIVIDUAL FORM OF BIRTH,
my BABY........ SEEKED A VERY INDIVIDUAL OUTCOME
TO HIS BIRTH! right into Donald Land.

THAT WAS MY VERY INDIVIDUAL FORM OF BIRTH,
my BABY........ SEEKED A VERY INDIVIDUAL OUTCOME
TO HIS BIRTH! way into it SHIT!

If the place for your child, where it grows up now,
there is no better place than one, where drugs are sold like fish,
Mothers are sold like fish, and cured like eel,
where children generally hardly have to attend school,
because coming home pregnant at 11
so more children at night walking through streets irritated, disoriented,
or they are gigantic in size,
even before graduating from school,
where children generally have fun consists of MOBBING,
and the END GOAL of a primary school at the level,
who will be next take his life in class?

THESE FINE, LOVELY CHILDREN
are given their Abitur just so they can finally leave !
Then you know how much sense lullabies have here !

Who in the country is getting their hands dirty
when our children are born, for highly paid people,
whose hands are now covered in blood?
The killer argument today is, why think about it,
when there is a gaming addiction?
Do we shoot the zombies, and then ask
our mothers whether we did a good job?
BECAUSE OF HALOWEEN and all that?
NARCISSISTS and LOSERS !

Historical correction for stupid crap:
December 29, 1890, Massacre and Battle of Wounded Knee

Fall of the German Wall: November 10, 1989 Freed from a dictatorship

1975 American Independence:
This war was triggered by the North American colonies'
efforts to gain independence from the British crown.

November 5, 2024 Possible overthrow by the fascists:
Rightwindgs attempts to overthrow the 400-year-old democracy

For every patient in Germany a separate LAW !!
The Relief Act, for old age and dementia, through the rigorous authority
of the financial world, to the point of incapacitation !

The Financing Act,
for the exploitation of the little citizen, and to enable private and noble
people to continue their privileged life !

The Teeth Act,
for the official purpose of taking the breath away from women,
who are often raped and dumped somewhere,
who believe that all their teeth are falling out,
and refusing to give them identity papers !

The Old Age Bankruptcy Act,for the expropriation of apartments or houses,
in order to obtain real estate easily and cheaply !

The Sat-1 midday program law, for the purpose of tactic of lulling those
who willingly bow to the law ! I just mentioned Hal Foster's
"Who's Afraid of the Neo-Avant-Garde?" to me apropos this tweet.
"There's both no knowledge of art history beyond superficial canonical
images and the underlying philosophy of earlier artists".

She notes. "They are therefore not able to respond with something new and innovative that is a response but also a continuum of artistic creation. An example would be Abstract Expressionism but also a unique visualisation of those artists' engagement phenomenology."

There is, I think, a meta-complication, which is the relationship of both the imitators and the audiences to history itself. There's more than ignorance involved. As with all art, and 'art', there is a worldview and a circumstance that is unique and fundamental to this particular form of gnostic [re]production. It has something to do with compressive expression, the new media we are using, the relationships it fosters and emergent, immersive forms of spectacle and spectator. We have a small group of kindreds investigating these issues in a group.

The hardcore lone fighter.... is someone whose mouth
opens and closes again, his brain soaked in gin, tie, turquoise silk shirt,
the cellar full of quirks, always the smile of a winner, only makes promises,
cuts off all other ideas with nakedness,
castles in the air and schemer that he is,
softened in the brain because he is not at all potent,
simply shows off his best friends in front of everyone,
until everyone knows it, an asshole, but nothing behind it,
because he is not cooperative, and in the end equally unsuccessful !

I once read that water is a symbol of emotions,
and for some time I've been thinking that I might drown in both.
~ Jessi Kirby

Don't be ashamed, share life with a friend
and have known each other for a long time,
to give them a feeling of security and safety
to welcome them into the family
to share your children and give gifts, to guarantee to just take it.
Learn from every other living being.

When a quarter of the doctors here have now gone abroad.
When right-wingers sit on talk shows here, right-wingers make jokes.
When in the sinking boat, the men are the first to be asked,
the ones who go under, the strangers, the children, then the women.
When in retrospect there aren't many left,
the Porsche drivers, the precocious ones, are just as much the ones
who will go under in this form of EVOLUTION.

Well, the man has screwed up here, how we need new men !
Where are they supposed to come from?
If the women already say no. If the women look around.
If they can only endure the horror of man.
We still know that running away is never the solution,
it only tightens the noose around all of our necks,
if you no longer look your friend in the eye
and accept him, there will be no way out !

Just imagine, taking the noose from one person's neck,
putting a splint on another's broken nose,
forgiving another's losses, smiling at another's failure, forgetting another's
embarrassment, and everyone is left without water ! Once a year, Germany
loses as much water as the entire Lake Constance, the devastation in the
country is the greatest in the world. And so they finally sit down at the table
together after their last beer, realizing that it doesn't matter who we all were,
but only who we all are right now ! and working together for a future in
which we create something together by using what we have. Lots of fresh
air, little water, and freshly brewed filter coffee !

This meant, we have enough of all the psychopaths
who are just waiting for peoples fall, do not wonder, if world won't heal by
the special crap, that will never anybody learn !

It's good to go to bed early, yeah, I know how it is, except that just at the moment when someone is really about to go to sleep, someone rings the bell and wants something, and you ask to go outside, and you can see that it's over, but if you don't want to, then you've already... if you know that you're talking to me, you'll eventually have the courage to come over again, that's really sinking in. Because it's a lovely evening. I've finally made a start and since yesterday I've declared four women friends, it's all going really well.

The FAMILY MOUTH does not reveal the truth.
The business is criminal. The woman needs money, the edge of the bed, a kitchen for her husband, children to fuss over,dog that gets the hate, gray-haired dachshund. The woman also needs self-centeredness, for the sake of mendacity, ignorance, concealing the kicks that are dished out,
FAMILY LIFE can be lived without problems!
The CONDITIONS are always there for it. The temptation of money, can withstand strong people, the temptation of power only the saints.

THE EGO - MUSTER gets his money's worth !
Come on in, you can admire me, that people are pleasure-seekers!
Only the good ones, if at all, would be allowed to use my coffee machine.
Only the handsome ones, if at all, would have a career after the model year.
Only the girly type, if at all, has to be a bit stupid, every hit chart guarantee.
Only the hip ones have their privileges,
who don't have to clean a hip machine, but simply buy a new one.
Only the chilled sparkling water from the tap, changed life they discovered.
Only the smart house knows its updates, the orders in advance optimize life.
Only the air conditioning unit makes camping fun, the smart house does the shopping, and every now and then paints a picture just for themselves.

A celebrity created "art", sold for horrendous sums.
A purchased ready-made canvas. Adhesive tape to mask off the surfaces, mixed a couple of colors, slapped on like in elementary school, copied and added spontaneously, and then let Chat GPT choose the title, GPT can also provide any interview questions.

Good has no connection to authenticity, as in the real art world,
referring to any existing style, working method, known painting style,
composition, justified reference to an era, but the copied children's gossip
version wants to be branded and sold as "art".

What is there not to understand about that?
When a little daughter experiences total rejection from her family?
When she looks for friends and like-minded people
at every possible way out of the dilemma?
When she brings such a friend home three times to introduce him, the sisters
are fucking their friends in the parental home, but she is blessed, for trying
to have a friend 3 times, she is beaten out three times in "disgrace", i.e.
simply driven into homelessness as a child, then raped three times during
this family "experience" of defenselessness. This had the educational
intention to drive love out of her for self-protection reasons, in order to
protect her from "worse" things, and thus also to "treat" her in captivity.
The means to do this is violence. A family's "cry for help"! Like father's fake
deodorant, a total rejection of all, whoever smells like that.
"I have white mice and rum pot in the basement"
"I eat boiled eggs in the office and breathe cigars"
"I cut my toenails at the kitchen table
on a blue, black and white wax tablecloth"

and yet father only wanted to wear the name Goebbels on her vest,
whereby the little daughter spends her whole life wishing for a deodorant
that smells like a "smellable full-body condom",
remembered like "an estrogenic protective shield"
"that's eternal virginity in a can" but if father were to smell it so constantly,
that's why she would run away from him all her life, so he will never find
Mrs. Goebbels in his daughter!

Keep smile ! Don't worry ! Be happy ! The most wanted wish,
to live in a dictatorship. The most wanted wish.
Say goodbye like a pro !

THE GUARDIAN OF THE MANURE HEAP!

You will be amazed at what a humus heap can produce!
people go to church, confess to their father not in his name,
drink a free drink for confession, have oldies evenings with records,
or a dance for back exercises, no matter how ridiculous gymnastics is,
how dirty their pants are, who fart without being ashamed,
in nice brown polyester pants.... offer their cocks under their robes.
Who like to "come" in this way. So we leave it at that, that's why the young
leave, why very few get married, they don't want to "come" in this way ?

We look at the year and the finish, the taste of her life,
the physical backwardness and the connection to her lifestyle
that remained of this has its smell, and judging by the smell,
I can assume to what extent physical and above all mental state is now,
and how that compares to people who have died today !
SHIT HAPPENS.... no one talks about it, because the characteristic of
every village is its sole BODY LANGUAGE.

When she's pregnant ! and he dreamed in the distant future of
showing the world what he was made of, but he's got nothing to give !

THE PHYSIO THERAPIST ADVISES!!

Would you rather, in order to be taken seriously, not inflict pain on yourself?
That is what your doctor or pharmacist recommends! Research has shown
time and again that people seek out their pain, and from this it can be
concluded how the drug can be used to counteract it, simply take the opiates
orally, exactly like that !

The hammering and stabbing as acute pain, neuropathic, chronic pain,
which will change if you continue to take the drug
with 100% guarantee as a symptom
to the special experience caused by addiction
can be increased to immeasurable reach !
SO have fun with it, wishes your doctor or pharmacist !

Forced to live in a reality that does not match our feelings.
Sometimes we wish our dreams were real.
And sometimes we wish our reality was a dream.
We leave our reality with boxes of dreams.
And then we grow up and our dreams fall like autumn leaves.
This is our life, a dream that comes true and a dream that stumbles.
And our dreams remain waiting, a path between reality and patience.

Yeah that is like the real good ones of aquaintances outside, you never
guessed to find, never know, but may happen that your innerst wish came
true within hours, as a gift of your fate, and everybody envolved is as happy
as me ! yes, our credo is the saying "You will from now on just make the
best out of your time coming !" yourself in the dark cave, that is the reason
why i use old stoff, too, i am not spilling my time and money for that, have a
good time, tonight in the winter cave, romantic warm, and take the chance
to feel good in order to just make the best feeling out of it in this time.
I can't explain myself why that does not function with my Art, because
nobody ever asked me for this ? But i believe that nowadays the Art world
changed to an illegal stealing and robbing of wisdom all kinds. I am pretty
sure that the mass of worlds of me since about ten years were all good stoff
to build up other people, it is like you say, but almost all of them only
contacted me one after another in order to push me out their ways, bully,
trigger, fear me, leave me standing with empty hands, ghosting me, and
collecting many real presents that i sended to them privatly, then laughing at
me and let me feel very abused in trust. They even still call back to me, in
order to ask me for money or more. I was too often feeling like a bad treated
dog.

And d i rested in sorrow how really evil that people show up.
a miniplay: Wait a minute, tick tock, i thought you were a man of your word
not with criminals and politicians?
not with pollluters what about teachers?
not with blondes or the world or cartoons or clowns
tick tock what about the arrogant + stupid? your clothes speak loud + clear

Plato says: If someone ignores you, they are asking you to leave their life.

While Shakespeare said: "If someone ignores you, know that you are the most important thing to them."

What is more correct in your view?!!!!!!!!

It is the former. It is as certain as the amen in church.
Those who live self-centeredly, picture LOVE as an illusion,
they have a hollow, pale form of it in their minds,
far from reality, even paranoid, more than a wishful thinking,
caught up in narcissism, wrapped up,
these people never greet anyone, they radiate an aggression
that makes them doubt their existence, like an electric rage in their posture,
ignorant of how they are seen by others, high degree psychopathic violence
TAKE CARE OF YOURSELF !

Exactly, that applies to EVERYONE. We are going through a difficult time, it's no wonder that I only meet very confident, clear-headed people at the moment, it seems appropriate for everything that is going on and everyone is wide awake. Some days you have the most obvious thoughts about a certain type of people, and then you meet them and it happens as expected, only that you laugh about it together. When I observe that general caution has led even older people to draw the conclusion, emphasized in the "times", that they do not want any approach from those who are mentally impaired, whose noble homes are not tolerated, over whose gates you can now see white and red barrier tape, which allows one to draw conclusions about how the fine people of today think, even though their noble house is almost in the middle of hospital complex, and the homes all around them, I mean, really, what have the weakest in society, whom they despise so much, done to these rusty old people when things get tough? That's why I am far from thinking that old people are "good", animals have always been far more honest to me, ALL of them.

72

Who says that a project, a club, a clan, like the fascist clan
or something similar... is addressed, I'm not someone
who is easily tempted by a peanut bar, but...
so that environmental crime is finally taken seriously by people?

Cooperation ! Is the way forward.
If everyone had to ingratiate themselves,
slide up on their knees, give the fat guy a big hug,
the matchmakers and spies, the snoopers and stereo bugs,
even the lonely country bumpkins, the monogamous and sycophants,
would actually have too much to do !
It can even be done without... greed, and thrift, without wiping your ass,
only focusing on yourself ! So, Am I seeing that correctly?
just for the sake of assumption... because of the woman
Work per se is not expected, and is not awarded as such,
oblige in front of the Oktoberfest Club of Bellies
like any political party from each of these to hold tightly to you
and let it hold until it turns blue, so that it also plays a "main" role,
and thus, as a consolation, get cleverly fit,
will stand up again in the fitness center?

IT IS REALLY A PLEASURE FOR ME
TO SHAPE EUROPE TOGETHER WITH YOU - THANK YOU!
THE AUTHORITY Through EUROPE
FIGHTING ENVIRONMENTAL CRIME is a FACT!

The woman first goes alone the path of the expectant mother,
yes, the female to be protected, whose body now doubles,
stretches and expands, the tissue tears, thinking falters, she sees the stars,
and generally only lies there naked in bed, just like that, she only wanted
to be held in the arms of her Earl out there in battle, anxious that her knight
would give his life for them all! She moans, sweats, eats the fridge empty,
they had barely spoken of children when the first was almost born, she must
be the hottest mare of all time for him !

AHHHHH WILLIAM, come ride home at last !
Ah, it always had to be him who got dressed first, then finally he just said,
"Darling, I just have to go and get some cigarettes, wait for me !"
the lover lay there for nine months, she waited, the lover, nothing happened.
Close the window that hurts you, no matter how beautiful the view.

Quietly, every door that closes at the will of its owner,
never knock on it...
These won't call you back,
who invited you in order to shout at you.
These won't feed the guest,
who deny come close to a sister.
These won't hide to blame you,
even in front of your children for nothing.
These choleric types,
who are willing to harm even physically.
These feel no sorrow,
all that they wanted is your ART, and you give it to them !

A person who is sold, no matter how much his price is, will remain cheap...
Meet situations with similar situations, do not blame anyone.

I THINK THE LAPIDAR SAYING
"COME IN MY BOAT!" is therefore irrelevant !
EXPRESSED LAPIDARLY - LACONIA

Imagine, that pregnant, bleeding, acutely endangered
WOMEN stayed away from the doctor and died !
Imagine, the latest EPIDEMIC, many die from indifference, sees it as a
project to provide men with all "security", and WOMEN give birth to all the
children of rape ? Imagine, the male clientele hypocritically brought about
these conditions, because they CHOSE it !
Even when I wanted to escape the whole world, you to come with me.
Who still uses the mental muscles of their own children?

Who shows it by smoking in the car?
Who leaves the children in the car while shopping?
Who sends the little ones to school alone?
Who lets their child go out with strangers in the dark?
Who sends their child to hit back?
Who lets their child make their way through school?
Who publishes what goes wrong at school?
Who denounces the first murder case in their community?
Who sends their child to leave the city?
Who sees their child find their way in America, Sweden
and even in Ukraine?
Who tolerates their child gaining poor professional experience?
Who sometimes argues with their child?

Caesar must also have said... during the assassination
"In Vino veritas!" or something like that.......
"You can all kiss my ass, including you, my son Brutus".

General Custer - and other idiots
Little Bighorn River, USA, June 24, 1876
Relevant people: the Native Americans!

The phenomenon reflects unity. That's why I stop the world, experience is
the best way to gain knowledge, to see. To walk a path in a fair way.

USA PARENTS' DAY in the STONE AGE,
so no more school, the "teacher" speaks at the campfire:
first cave paintings discovered as graffiti, accusation used black charcoal on
the rock that can hardly be washed off, everything is at an end!
Doctors in the "West" complain about ridiculousness, they say their motto is
"All for one, and one for all ...." or something like that, BUT unless you
yourself are in danger and it is not worth putting yourself in danger!"

The necessary tension and dynamics
of the raped women in the future, should be reminded, please,
thanks to the paedophile, the abusive father,
the choleric men on duty, with certainly sadistic tendencies,
their victims should please, for the video presentation,
at best also stick to the text ! That is also what the "Amen in church" says!
one wants it to be said decently.

My friend said on the phone, that things really should not have happened in
this my life, but now it is allright what to tell about the States and all true,
but max nix, he said, this is like the germans in WWII all did, they chose
that fate by politic, now the States of America ! They will quickly reflect on
what they did, and enter in their deepest mood when wanting to choose
another way again, but that's theirs to do !

What could we do ? We could just go with posters to the Schlei waterarm
and stand there protesting against, but NONE and really nobody would take
any notice of it !

The Finish Line – Last Step !
This is the first step of all drowning, when ignorance has filled the space,
then all chaos, intolerance and stress will take part,
where was familiar life, everyone finds his own ego in the middle,
every ego is the credo of survival, every searching for a find out,
is paired with the hurting of others, the accu empties, the good seed is gone,
when the divide, the divorce has started, when sex is just a reason
to get the stick out. This is the moment when people realize in front of the
own children, that the first start of love is an ideal, the second space has
opened for all other possible ideal ways to see,
then compare them, and see, the reality, the problems within.
And nobody likes realizing the problems, not those of others,
not the own, not to confront, and not to change any situation,
not to just take a calm step behind.

Courage is not the lack of fear, courage is moving forward while being afraid. A friend who waits for a misunderstanding to destroy a relationship is actually an enemy..!!! Don't be like those stupid dogs who think people are afraid of them when they bark, when in reality the dogs who bark are afraid.

If I have met at least. Fourteen people in my life who tried to take me on, in truth in the name of friendship, trying to let me fall for whatever it was that wanted to destroy a relationship, whatever it was,
then I know I have indeed seen many corpses float down the river,
and let fourteen people fall on themselves
who were not friends in the least, but enemies.

Now it's time for coffee and warm thoughts, I feel like laughing a little more than usual today. When we came out of the forest, someone ran towards us with a tiny, round, super cute pug, I waited to see if the big, round eyes spoke to me in a loving way, and then, I tell you, we spontaneously fell in love. I can still imagine the owner walking through the big natural forest with his Ricky pug, and the pug today with the biggest declaration of love ever in his little luggage, that must have been touching! I know that from my own dog, when love takes over like that, you can really see dogs grow wings.

It's my birthday in three or four days, and as always, no one is there, because I've often tried to invite people to dinner at events like this, and I was actually sitting there all alone while preparing and eating, they didn't even have the courage to tell me on the phone that they didn't want to come! Last year, the same thing happened, then I dreamed about the idiot and a race track that I won as the runner, his little dog Kessy then praised me in my dream and said that her secret name was actually Krümel, and I woke up, but the guy and his dog just told me outside that it just happened that evening that he now had a new girlfriend, and I answered him about the fact. The women in my dream told me about him, "At least it was worth trying!" But the a-hole got a proper "trip" on a trip on the city road with his new fuck machine. Based on these facts, pizza for Heike alone this year !

I know why? You're never really alone, there are always new people you meet for the first time outside and they have a lot of fun with you, just as you pass by, and you just look each other in the eye and suddenly you're happy again! Whether you have a job or not, I know that you know exactly what I'm talking about! Sleep well and dream something nice, maybe about a vacation in the Maldives with some beautiful divas.

People...
are the worst for me.
The animals...
are my only true friends.
The birds...
are related to our language.
The wolves...
are the mediators of all wisdom.
The forests...
are the preservers of all life.
The children...
will no longer be born in the future on earth !

Choosing a man doesn't just depend on whether he eats his sausage without making a mess. She doesn't tell him when you first meet whether and how much she messes up during her period. You can still feel lonely in a relationship and don't see it as a problem to like each other even when you're apart, because you also dream in all sorts of bright colors and your heart beats warmly. We need people with common sense here. I won't want the man who thinks that I'm too old for him, as if I'm always horny and need someone like him in life like I need a crankshaft for a car, because I don't expect anyone to improve in life and because I don't need pity sex. I know that a large number of men see women as a useful object, whose value decreases when they are "purchased", just as a new car has already decreased its "value" by €10,000 when it goes on sale. This is how many people see it in relation to the value of women, the so-called "used" ones are less suitable, and to be honest, with old cars too, there is always something!

What does a person want to say? A lot for sure, if they dare to say something, which is more important than the "value" of a conversation, because there is also a special meaning hidden behind the words. A relationship of any kind depends on accepting someone as they are, embracing a person with all their experiences.

Expectations are often not fulfilled. Some people are not suited to a relationship. It is the everyday little things, the other person fails to meet their own expectations, everyday life, the routine slips away until the bomb explodes, then the lights go out in a relationship.

The woman wants to be respected.
She needs fatherly care. She needs to feel wanted.
Her desire for the big harbor tour is always there.
She loves being the center of attention.
But then the "shine wears off" early on.
The ideal is replaced by hopelessness.
Two people who grow old together separate in death.
The memory of each other fades, nothing remains.
They felt eternally loyal like two swans, until the day
when he drunkenly shit in the family's living room at Christmas
and Santa Claus had to clean it up. One day the woman took him to a hut to get rid of the alcohol or die from it. Then he was dead.

I admit, I consider this family monster to make it clear to me, to the victim, that many of the abusive events should not have taken place. No one had the courage to apologize to me on behalf of everyone. But I can see, even in everyone's eyes, that they know that I have had a moment where I wished my father died, I admit that. I am certain that the longer they put off confronting me, the further away they are from living true happiness in their lives, because only those who know how to make others happy will experience happiness in return, and I wouldn't want to be in their shoes!

This was linked to my father, from whom running away was the only, the ONLY, way to escape the disgust, because in life every fat bastard insists on meeting the women he buys and grinning while doing so with money and yet escaping without punishment !

A little tree on the left, A little tree on the right,
A stream flows in the middle, Oh!!!

Why are there unique men living among us today
who imagine that they know what women need
after a rape, because they have the only true solution?
I can't answer that, I fled with all four wheels
under my saddle as far away as I could, and started my life anew,
and I spent sixty years dealing with it, ALONE!

This was one of my ART PIECES, that i destroyed, made a silly copy, sended it to a handicapped cousin, and was fed with it at last !

People who search one to listen to a huge health problem, someone has any problem, and you only see his death, you are pretty weird friend. The first two sentances you tell about a beloved person, a family part, your sentances speak about someone gone, and lost with the wind, dead and vanished all over. I said, if i told you such a truth, i would better not wait for that moment when you react in mourning about the other. Maybe this is people's problem, to talk to all others with huge problems, have the socalled language to talk to skeletton people like speaking to the bones. These are people who are afraid of reality. They fear to speak things out, and confront to what is around them, then only search for contacting those who are deadly sick and almost gone, then the going deeper into an issue is not needed anymore.

Now i understand 100% turn away from me, let me fall like a hot potatoe, then asit in any kinda marriage party, and just show one sick guesture to drink with drunkyard friend and fall behind.

You have to be able to be generous. You could read series to learn how a writer like me came to express, with great passion, my deeply precious need to free myself, to leave the emotional limitations of my mentally ill parents behind, 2 Understanding Human Nature and Part 3 Cutting the Cord !

What should children do.....? and what shouldn't they do!!!!
A child only learns what it wants. I'm sooo sick of this question.
Send the children off, break their legs run around,
throw them in the water to drown, let them go swimming,
and you drink red wine on the bank, pretend you have to laugh about it,
don't ask which 10 meter high tree the child is calling you down from,
don't worry, slide on a board pulled behind the boat,
be able to balance between treetops, in some scree slopes on peaks,
get their bike repaired, listen to the eagle complain about them.

What kind of relationship will last.
The sin arises when the guy,
even after the relationship started,
sweet and cheap, greeted the neighbor at the checkout,
who was really sorry for my rotten teeth,
a couple has broken up on holiday.
It's face to face, with the motto
"It's good that you're here, I wanted to tell you something!"
In this case it's "in order to make a good choice, it's over"
Love in fact, REAL love, cannot and will not die, my dears !
Now that's a controversial topic, for example
"I had sex with someone nice one evening in my parents' bed!" no problems
with that, but I wouldn't do something like that the other way around.

What is that supposed to be a sin? Farting and being ashamed?
Never. I would have blamed it on the baby forever,
it's not worth mentioning, ultimately irrelevant as a sin.

Today it is said.... accept the future INHERITANCE,
see yourself celebrated, put your feet in front of each other,
sweep in front of the door, bend down, mow the lawn,
but to inherit tax-free 2,000,000
so that you can finally make the whole Thailand happy !
and learn like a woman you appreciate instead of "desiring"
or respecting her, if you eat,
I'd no longer serve food to every palate!

I do have a claim to artistic work, which is why, as a woman,
I do not offer my art just as a "favor", a "Big Mac" everyone should like,
so that it becomes a "business idea", what I do is a whim,
the story of how it came about counts,
because I only eat something quick at home,
and quickly without an audience, "God forbid invite anyone to dinner!"
let them feed their children alone.

What's erotic painture ?
Is it the feeling while painting ?
Is it the congruence with nature ?
Is it the musician in your veins ?
Is it the connected proximity to dreams ?

The cow in the morning, slurps coffee without a care,
wants to borrow a pencil, to provide her ideas with vision.

Waiting doesn't happen every day, it won't bring fulfillment,
someone to drive away your loneliness,
but to look you in the eyes, even if only to survive,
it is the idyll that never existed !
Good One hahaha therefore i destroyed it.

LIGHT HOUSE
The total isolation. The chosen empty love.
The search for proximity. The deadline for the past.
The therapy for faults. The rescue for cold hearts.
The ignorance of friendly words. The fear of climate change.
The none existance of perception. The siro dialog to the world.
The handicap for decades. The signal to change the path.
The origin apologize to elderly. The insightful realize to start anew.
The take your time, to better leave.

The picture like two people in one boat
I see it the same with skulls and T-shirts with that,
this is modern superflous crap,
this shocking the people see that,
this is disrespectful to soft minded,
this is the short cut to hide them,
that your inner balance was never found,
these skeleton appearances of confronting,
those who are definitely not prepared,
there is nothing to say but that,
but the skeleton people looking for their kick!
I have that in mind, tomorrow we'll drink!
I know the walk around it, when the bellies are full.
I'm on guard against the old people, who sing as if they were young,
who go into the field and even turn completely green when they vomit,
whose gait staggers along the street, when the bus is already filling up,
while they make circles with corn, with Dörthe, who is so blonde,
and whose long hair is so lovely.
I thought to myself, that's the model,
she's missing a hat,
and the wool from Mother Holle,
then she won't let her fingers rest.
So tomorrow I'll celebrate my 60th alone !
It's just occurred to me tomorrow !

Prominent characters and mainstream,
bad luck for euphorics, your sex change would also be a business model,
although who is harmed by too much of a prong?
Good idea, that thing with the stumbling blocks!
My only German and of course best German friend in this area,
whose dad also finally received his stumbling block, in the last few years,
after applying for it to be made public in relation to
his resistance movement 65 years ago!
My friend had almost really had enough!

People, parenthood is abolished !
No chance of survival for the two of them,
in terms of work or children,
in terms of colleagues or friends,
in terms of Mother Courage or kindergarten,
in terms of marriage or social welfare,
in terms of church or slavery,
in terms of studies or sex,
in terms of child benefit or homelessness,
in terms of too many students.
No one who can do anything will flood in,
and then they will disappear to the beautiful city,
because the fine people will soon have careers,
there are too many concerns in the country !

Back in the Stone Age - at the patent office:
I ask "Can I patent my ability to think?"
the official: "Bring me a dead skunk, you can use that better!"
and pushes me along, "Next please!"

TO THE WOMEN DEFEATERS -
"FROM ONE SHORE TO THE OTHER!"

One night the sea died,
from one shore to the other, folding, shrinking,
a cloak that is taken away.
Like a drunken albatross,
like a fleeting predator,
it ran with ten waves
to the farthest horizon,
when the bereaved world saw the light of day again,
the sea was a broken horn,
no longer answering the call.
We fishermen went down to the desecrated shore,
it lay there wrinkled and bare.

Martha had the poem by Gabriela Mistral, the Chilean Nobel Prize winner
for literature in 1954, tattooed on her young back.

Be nice to each other ! Yeah, I can agree with you there,
the more polite you are, the harder you have to try !
It's no detriment to introduce yourself by name !
I just don't want to be called "You look much younger than 60 !"
on my birthday, just because their women are always pestering me for that !
I'm still not from another planet, am I ?

Why should people always strive to live forever?
If only we ... could stop from eating Crackers jellied with sugar,
the cigarette smoke on a stick, sold egg liqueur, to live a happily long life?
What is the point of being stingy? Do they always want us
to impregnate ourselves, to clean up the mess,
to get rid of the children's shit, to get rid of the routine,
to be happy with the same old everyday life, when there is also an option
to simply be happy and just spread our legs???

The President advises... Women are not doctors, but nurses,
like to look stupid, are sometimes just out of date.
Women are married, more like starving anorexic, to get laid.
Women don't like studying, dancing until the doctor comes is in their blood.
Women don't have the courage to give birth,
so they deliver the brood with the hands of doctors,
that keeps them thin and on to the next
person who wants to make the empty nut fat again !
Men always said that being women was something that
when a woman is a woman - it's hardly up to her!

Super Manni, you take a quick sniff around,
where there is a fire, that's where you are needed,
you can't cook, you can't get toast golden brown,
you're not tall when you go out,
how could you, dwarves can barely manage it,
you've also gotten a bit fat, but then you take another sniff,
where is the fire still burning? Oh, it's Lorenz Otto's old granny,
she's stuck under the curler cap, totally alone and distraught,
while the master hairdresser in charge
loses the overview while fucking,
and doesn't even pay attention to her,
Tss Tss there you see again, Manni has to step in here,
Lorenzo Otto's old granny is waiting, he has to pick up the pace,
but how does the story continue, while Manni asks God,
if he needs his cough drop, and everyone has to get out of the way,
but it was a close call, says God. Under the motto
"Dare to be more democratic!" Mrs. Brandt from the office
works every day from Monday to Friday, except Tuesday, when she is ill,
she is close to the system, who accept such stuff from their backlog of files
that are piled up to the ceiling, that the needy are recommended to use to
win a ticket from the church lottery with the bonus point,
like taking pregnant women's children away at birth!

The child learns early on how it feels,
what is said, "Finger in the bum, that's just how it is!"
To keep their mouths shut and threatened to publish from now on,
the mothers are warned not to dare to look for paid work,
otherwise their pants will be pulled down, in the literal sense,
and a nice coercive measure on top of that, to add to the list of
discrimination, lawyers hold their bellies with laughter,
to make prostitution palatable, nicely in a church setting, of course!

'You stand in the sea like Aquarius, with your back to the waves, in the
spray up to your knees in the water, withstanding wind and water, trident in
hand, also covering the backs of many of your friends, ... but if you have to
get up early, you also go to bed early!' and THAT'S A GOOD THING!
grounded to a much better future with that awesome child !

Long-term single Dingeldu joins a tandem club
to find a new pearl, he drives a long bus
on a trip for singles excursions, and no one comes with him,
he says his coffee is a hit, because he knows that, if he finds someone
who likes to bend over in front of him, it's a real hit for the first hour,
his reason for this is drinking a lot of coffee,
because it's like love, you can't sleep at all because it's gone to his head,
so a girl with a gift for languages finally has to ring his doorbell !

Pussy Riot ! Adopted Home ! Then you're done, as they say in the far north!
The voyeurs, who offer strangers' children.
The hoarders, who make the surrounding houses available.
The gossips, who offer them the invitation to be eaten by rats.
The customers, who give birth to the latest form.
The thinkers, who read the bloodiest riot act.
The rat catchers, who help clip the wings of others.
The elegantly designed aristocratic, who create the perfect literary coffee
house atmosphere. The one-man party Hanseatics, who park their Ferrari in
front of the house.The writers, who steal their children and their pens.

The woman looks for variety in the disco,
at parties, in advertisements, many disabled siblings grow up,
and the man, who always finds himself on the outside,
realizes, "Oh, if only he had liked children better!"
We are in dark times, there are few true people.
The painting is the truth comes to light over time.
This is the Fleetwood Mac I like.
Deeply meaningful lyrics about the futility of life.
The music has that nostalgic tone. One of my favourite songs of all time.
Yes, I think her melancholic look and those colourful wings, a symbol of
transformation and she dares to daydream.

WRONG ROSALINDE !
I think the old woman, the sick one from above, came from Swabia,
where she was the only lesbian who voted conservative !
So she knows a thing or two about why she was excluded all her life.
She approaches people formally, even piously, as if she could only walk on
ice skates. She reported herself as a helpless person years ago,
she even spent 1000 euros to seal it, has always been mentally handicapped,
she even sings that in the church choir, at home with the difficult cases,
if only you can finally look behind her curtain !
I have had several interviews, were difficult, but some were successful.

First, I freed someone with dark skin from
the self-imposed ISOLATION situation.
Second, the interview helped someone to make the leap into a drug-free life,
and we have remained friends to this day.
Third, I helped someone through their dramatic back surgery,
he helped me to gain real self-knowledge.
Fourth, I almost managed to create a podcast that was internationally
recognized by and for art, and a sexist accusation against me evaporated.
Fifth, I solved every puzzle about autism, about my family history, about my
healing and about my past. I also contributed every insight into my life to
my 16 novels.

I was pressed down by someone sexist and that strange person, with name and birthdate exact like my father, he had sent me completely disgusting dick pics despite warnings against it, it had such a traumatizing effect on me I was already part of the core of The3NinesArts and had started a blog.

In 2004-2005 and between 2009-2014 I worked with disabled clients, i.e. physically or mentally impaired, and at the end I published a book about my reflections "social work with people with disabilities" german and english. In this work I also conducted numerous interviews with people, and at the time I designed fifteen of my own magazines for everyone as a thank you for their cooperation.

What's the difference between intellectual understanding and realization?

Realizing something causes a complete shift in perspective which then results in a permanent change in behavior - the way we act and react to life's experiences. When you realize the finiteness of time, the preciousness of life becomes profoundly evident, compelling you to deeply value each moment and live with greater clarity and intention. But you can't live intentionally if you lack clarity. Having a vision of the future is essential for creating the life you desire. A clear mental picture allows you to focus your energy precisely where it needs to go. After all, life is a manifestation of where you invest your energy. If you do not define a destination for your energy, rest assured, your environment will. Beyond knowing where to direct your energy, it's important to understand that everything is created on the mental plane before it manifests on the physical plane.

Start your day with silence. Find a peaceful spot to sit quietly, breathe deeply, and let your mind settle. Imagine your head clearing up, like clouds parting after a storm. This calm is your invitation for the new day ahead.

I wanted to walk around the lake once,
and stayed there for hours, found the way there alone,
sunk deep into the night, listened electrified to the toads,
which sounded like they were from the underworld,

wanted to drive to town in the morning,
have a piece of bread with cheese,
take a shower, have no one around me,

didn't want to belong to anyone,
I preferred to leave my best friends alone, to this day...
have no respect for those who "want to belong!" MOTHERFUCKERS !

How it works - Indian Heike? Oh, raped three times already?

How it works - Kikki from Norway?
Oh, already passed three jobs only under bullying?

How it works - beloved wife and mother?
Oh, now you also know what is meant by motherfucking?

How it works - neighbor and acquaintance?
Oh, you're asking me here, after only thirty years?

The German philosopher (Immanuel Kant) was asked:
What is the difference between law and morality?

He answered:
In law: a person is guilty when he violates the rights of others.
In morality: a person is guilty if he thinks about it.

I know as well as a kind of friend who isn't worth it, well known, that he broke with his love dramatically but even more than 20 years ago, i make the real thought, I draw the conclusion, with all those broken wings is a connection, and reliable friendship, a trusting, and an expectation to true respect impossible to be aware ! This is for guarantee a person, who would be stuck in a dangerous situation, and would fear to loose all, this person would seemingly cross your road and forget about it to help you out, you could even then move over to a Sicilian police office to ask for urgent help better ! But thought they were the best fuckers and knowers in the world.

DEAR CHILDREN ! KEEP YOUR HANDS OFF THE CRACK !

- or is it the jar of sausages, on grandma's kitchen counter,
she cleans the stairs day in and day out,
she cleans the floor and always keeps the windows open,
the strawberry champagne is always opened,
just for the daughter, the daughter should get the sausages,
the humor can be up to her, the daughter should pay for them too !

Unequivocally OUT!
In the future, I will consider my way of life, as well as my own path,
as I consider it to be right, to be important.
I will also withdraw a little from that, and leave the "love" in networks,
those who eat the sausage on their slice of bread,
how they want to eat it, and not get involved.
See this as help for self-help. Imagine that, the fact that I might not come,
may have a much greater effect, than if I were there.
I am not as weak as 73 people have unequivocally
HOPED in the last few years !

You can see it in the woman, the femme fatale suffers,
she never had a connection to her body, no, she beat it all her life in order to
then raise it to something higher! In my opinion, she is too coward to live!

Yesss, i keep on going. I am still a thinker, an emancipated woman, studied
in all that meant life! It happens more often than you would imagine....
Life has sun and moon, light and shadow, but the question always remains,
whether smoking is still healthy, whether it is be better to get off Instagram,
in which case I feel very sorry for the guy who didn't want,
couldn't, would, would have, should have, had to offer an influencer and
partner doll the dream man, it certainly wasn't difficult for her to report
publicly in advance about why it didn't work out, obviously I knew that too,
when two women like that made advances to me from afar,
heading towards me at high speed, faster than an ICE train,
no one could explain it to me either,
who hasn't had this experience of the flight reaction,
who isn't prepared to encourage neuroses, and flees from them,
doesn't say a salute to them, doesn't serve their own children on a platter,
and doesn't refrained from moving a single muscle in their presence !

El chiste cancela inhibiciones internas y reabre fuentes de placer. Es una
actividad anímica una placentera y socializada. Que requiere de un otro con
el que se tenga una amplia concordancia psíquica. - Sigmund Freud -

Humor beseitigt innere Hemmungen und öffnet die Quellen der Lust wieder.
Es ist eine lebendige, angenehme und gesellige Aktivität. Dazu bedarf es
eines anderen, mit dem eine breite psychische Übereinstimmung besteht. -
Sigmund Freud -

Humor cancels internal inhibitions and reopens sources of pleasure. It is a
lively, pleasant and socialized activity. That requires of another with whom
there is a broad psychic concordance. - Sigmund Freud -

L'humour annule les inhibitions internes et rouvre les sources du plaisir.
C'est une activité vivante, agréable et socialisée. Cela requiert un autre avec
lequel il existe une large concordance psychique. - Sigmond Freud -

WORKER with SOCIAL RELATIONS ! We can YOU
Let's be like YOU mal honestly.. You go like all of us
for low pay to work, that this State beyond,
out of our workforce for almost Nothing benefits,
offers our good conscience while one offered in Smile,
continuous smiling Transformation,
and that cannot take us a state, him with good example to go forward !
You see, without ever being used by you, I have come countless times,
it only takes my thought, and not a finger more, and the waterfall is more
overwhelming than any other person could have shown me.

If people are now allowed to consider their own gender as having been
chosen by themselves, what would happen if certain people, whose, in short,
stupid political behavior, would require a psychiatric report in order for
them to want to do something?

I realized, the conversation with almost every animal funcions to all the
time, and the otherwise intellectual ability to most humans lacks more than a
thinking brain can bear, so that i trust in the animal far the most. Animals are
totally physically aware ! my opinion those none verbal people with a huge
hate and feeling not the be treated fair enough, they push on all others,
because they hate their body the most. That seems very likely, all boxed in,
or have you ever seen a real hater with a social behaviour ? Indeed the hate
starts in themselves, the asocial behaviour is the symptoms they show.

Would I say such a real authoritarian old guy is a real hater?
He is a politican with a psychiatric almost demencia and deep rooted
selfhate, and very small selfworth, that he needs the power in his job, to fold
out his symptomatical hate pushed on the masses.

BIGGEST CONCERN is,
the probability at Christmas the chance of a PENIS BREAKAGE
will inevitably increase - how far away will we be...
from the coming technological CHANGE???

So who is dreaming of...?
a metallic glass fart to the back of a historic castle building,
for a whole 100 million euros paid in advance by the taxpayer,
based on the minimum rate...! instead to remove the chemical waste,
the toxic sludge on the banks, underground and also from the water,
deepen the harbor, restore the Seagull Island, build a climbing park next
village, and build an oriental brothel !!

Now watch the creature powerhungry climber.
In my work and in life I found that every single abusive person - scratch the
surface and there you have it - a frustrated and deeply unhappy five or six
year old. jou, if he would have had parents with responsibility for child
births, then he would easily first have started with a job in social work and
would have become a social useful person, but otherwise he is stuck in frust.

WE Have never said enough, the way we accept our looking and our
physical being, as well as we function in clearness and wiseness, without
shouting out loud or pushing the weaker, this way we know that WE are the
partly healthier than the haters, who are nationalist. NO HUMAN is legal,
sothen the narcisst may have a visit in Kongo and work for the leader there.
they may cut the potatoe in Africa for hungry African People.

Samsaara ! The endless portals of our mind remain undiscovered,
undefined like sparks of secret fire buried deep in heart's mire.
I heard from a friend of mine who lives next door that she has been really
enjoying doing night shifts for disabled people in a residential home for
years, as a single mother, okay, I could say to you now, then write 128
books, when you have so much time to sit around anyway, but there are also
books that don't have to be read...! and in every city I lived in, I loved
visiting the old people in the retirement home because they are the best,
nothing awaits them there anymore and they still keep their sense of humor,
but in the end they said that I had more of a talent for being an artist and
should go that way, and anyway I had to cry at every human loss, I mean,
how could they have got anything out of me?

I advise you, as everyone says, if you are so physically busy, to do regular exercises like abdominal, leg and bum exercises. It only takes 20 minutes at a time and it works wonders for your spine because it gets the muscles working for you, which keep the spine stable in its natural and healthy position, and therefore no nerves are pinched. Because once the pain starts, you have to train again despite the pain until the muscles do their important work on your back ! I hope you stay in the flow, my friend, and please hang in there! So I hope you never let your courage and sense of humor be stolen from you !

So just pay attention to occurrences such as physical pain, and then take it seriously, I know from experience that this is easily remedied if you as a musician are aware of the vibrations, they must also vibrate and flow in the body, this reduces the acute pain, can be handled with the light centers perceived from the seat up to the head, this can flow if you allow the healing flow of energy within you, affirming yourself, the pain will suddenly disappear almost in the blink of an eye, then you can start the gymnastics against the pain with initial effort, and in about three days you will be back on your feet again!

I am fine, the sun is missing, outside freezy, but it is good in here, and my old little dog asleep, while have had a rest food from the pott, and coffee, what ever on a Sunday the time always stood still. I have had Birthday on the last Monday, my 60th, and so at the evening phoned me my sonnyboy, Julian, talking with me one long whole hour and gratulated me from heart, he was overhvelming kindful on the phone. I did really that i met spontaneously really many very kind people the last week, just having the most relaxed and humorous talks, and sat twice in a little coffee bakery point it was empty place for me and Mable doggy so we drank coffee and a little roll to eat, that is a fact, that nobody in town was willing to contact me or visit me for a good meal, as usual, since more than 30 years.

You can't understand me,
I don't belong on your little pedestal,
if you crawl around under me,
it will take your whiskey load, avoid the statement,
which I'm happy to give you, so keep your shoes on,
and hold on to your women's rags,
folks, we're on HOLIDAY together,
and where the sun travels, it rises in the morning,
I'm actually quite nice, you don't have to understand me,
but "NO" means "NO"!
Not everyone who takes time for you... has nothing to do.

Not everyone who gives you one chance after another has a weak
character... The only war that no one sees is the war within yourself.
They say you choose the guests of your heart.
What is my fault if you are the colonizer? There are battles that the only
way to win is not to fight them in the first place. Many eyes that were
happy with love have been brought to tears by fate. Some come into your
life as a blessing, some as a lesson, so keep the blessing and learn from the
lesson. Find your comfort and don't blame anyone because everyone knows
what they are doing..

Religious lovers want to possess their target.
They know that the person is happy without the family.
There is a desire to fill this gap.
The person realizes that he has done something bad to his target.
Knowing that it must finally end.
The person affected was no longer happy in it.
All others involved in such a process
would know nothing at all about him.
The view of the outside world is severely restricted.
One can even carry out the corpses knowingly.
There is definitely blood on his vest.

The people who are good and friendly,
open-hearted, generous, for over 30 years people
have not been so nice here, but in the provinces
there is more envy and greed, the envy of my kindness
and the greed that I have more wealth
from the bottom of my heart than normal people.
Yes, if they are nice, you can also see them sitting alone,
they are usually the ones who sit alone in the cafes.
Have you ever tried listening to someone who is lying...
and you know the truth..!

Fuck No ! In that situation i held distance,
then went at him for a share, then he quit and stared to a woman,
her name was Keike, and I was also called Heike,
that was too much, that liar was immediately caught
in an iron grip on the arm, pointing out that he has a lady
waiting for him at home, and this for this reason, not to try again here !
„Fuck No ! I won't try it again" was the reaction later on in town.

Never judge anyone, everyone has a story..!! It's nice for them to think you
don't know anything while you have files for everyone inside you.

There is much of real good news in the world, in LinkedIn people from
journalism, publishers, and so on, when i post my thought several times and
ask special people for look at my website, or for help to become known,
maybe i will have a good job with this ! this is with news from all over the
place, and real intellectual people, i like it, today i posted three comments,
and show my account with advertising my Art. Like John from Manchester
said it right now, Twitter is like putting a message in a bottle and tossing it
into the ocean hoping that the right person somehow finds and reads it, i
said, I know and i did it with about 73 people in ten years, i am really fed
with it, someone ad a really hardneck to still keep on going talking to me
since so long.

How is an #opinion created?

For example, if I suggest all vanilla #icecream should be #violet, my opinion will be looked at with amusement. At first. ONLY if I motivate a certain critical number of people ("many") to share my opinion, it becomes relevant. But if this success is not enough for me?

If I want a #law that all vanilla ice cream MUST be violet? Then I have to do more. I need many many "voices" showing up in media posting violet vanilla (VV). I need a powerful face for my campaign, and an organization "VVP Health" and some party members to support it.

A little bit of product placement. To get all this in place, I need money. For the next #elections there will be VV with the flag, national anthem, people with happy faces. And all of a sudden, if a "felt majority" supports VV I will win the election. Note: It all must FEEL like a majority. Very #many Social Media Accounts must post VV ice cream.

I do not real people AT FIRST. I only need to #simulate MANY on your smartphone. Then, after a while of #learning real people ("natural persons") will follow my opinion. People follow what they learned, saw, heard often enough. A completely natural human group behavior. People believe what the SEE, HEAR, and are TOLD often enough. And then I, you, everybody will think - hey, that is my opinion !

Welcome to the beautiful new world of #Violet #Vanilla!

LET HER GO! militant family breakfast prayerful thanks for the presents daughter athletic, intelligent, hardworking at school, doesn't complain, doesn't say much, is nicely dressed, the boys in the club have weapons in their hands, the girls are running Indian princesses, unpunctuality means unreliability, insults until their marathon is over one morning.

Super Manni called mom from the kitchen you take a quick sniff where it's burning, that's where you're needed, she believes from her husband.

But as the years go by, you can't cook, you can't get toast golden brown, the hut is dusty, stuffed animals in the shade, the furs are old, the feathers are shaggy, the hunt is over.

Parents argue, expose themselves in front of the audience,
she despises every man because her age says so,
you don't have any size when you go out, how could you,
dwarfs can hardly make it, she sees the man in the doorway.

The years have turned yellow like the wallpaper,
and only arguments, you've also gotten a little fat,
but then you smell it again, breakfast bacon is now burnt,
and the daughter recently ran away.
Where else are you burning if not in your heads?

Who a girl that just wanted to get out, viewed at an extreme,
out of mother's pub, away from father's obscene behavior,
away from biblical heels, away from the drunkenness and stench,
without the longing looks, the ugly advances,
because .... they all expect their little bit of gratitude from the girl,
the family entrusts her with keeping the peace of the family in the future,
and not attending any funerals, better still, leaving the family alone.
Girl grows out of a hateful desert!

A village community like this is like... a closed world,
with walls that are higher, with rocks along the streets,
with the silence of the lambs, with a castle dungeon outside the bedroom,
with pastors who drink, with passers-by who say nothing,
with neighbors without actions,
with looks that guess what belongs in their file,
but what the individual swears, what kind of friends daughters have,
what is enough for the gravestone,
that says "Gone with the wind,"
where everything revolves around the man's navel !

ALL PROBLEMS, the men have come from a system that favors men,
because it makes them rulers, but also because of that forces into the role
of rulers, in the role of strong, invulnerable, fighters who were actually
badly injured, extremely desperate boys remained,
Providers, nurturers, protectors, who have no weaknesses,
and who are not allowed to show feelings,
in the role of people, who can't do all that, or don't even want to.
And then you would rather kill yourself than say, man, that hurts !
In the manufacture of bread, the wheat is separated from the chaff, so in
human relations it is necessary to separate the elect from the called.

Every encounter ... a male expression i see, no single let it be, only the
power to go straight ahead, because this is man who does.
If a woman actually lived without, someone wants to know,
a horrendously bad home, a memory always caught up with her throughout
life, if she was basically run over by a train three times,
got up again from a thousand years of torture, to escape the life of her body,
if this tortured woman becomes pregnant, finds the father is no good for it
because he is violent and an alcoholic, a sleazy law as total transparency
about knowing who the father is would go one step further for the woman,
robbing her of her intimacy and precisely because this knowledge leads
to even more violence in the wrong person !

In my opinion: The man is paradoxical, and humanly speaking,
not someone you can really rely on in times of danger.
Whoever actually spent half his childhood with the female variant
always bathing together in the tub at almost 40°C,
in other words sharing the feelings,
the privilege of growing up with the woman,
but turns this down because of the privilege, out of fear
of losing a "freedom", of taking her side,
the privileged apparently sees the "greatest danger" in "freedom"!

In a multi-party landscape,
the individual from a decadent party
can benefit from staying in an expensive hotel
for all events, because society allows it.
In a majority of the population
In some places the individual may arise
for the decadent his special position
in the Sunday roast, festive mood, tax haven,
So everyone individually works underpaid,
so that the decade goes well again.
In our society, the majority, the individual,
often comes up short when it comes
to fair distribution between the top and bottom !

In other words sharing the feelings,
the privilege of growing up with the woman,
but turns this down because of the privilege, out of fear
of losing a "freedom", of taking her side,
the privileged apparently sees the "greatest danger" in "freedom"!

Without groove there is no move, with Art can the WORLD be changed,
where there is singing, take a seat, not the songs of fascists,
but ours, the much better ones ! Thank you very much !

Mr. Daddy ! and when you think it can't get any more stupid,
but then comes..., the one who sees them hanging on the cross,
not as locals like Jesus, but bed, bread, shit for refugees,
and he puts posters on them in camps of their origin that is Bavarian !
Be careful when you follow the masses,
sometimes the masses are at a loss for words!
No one has the right to simply let people drown
in the Mediterranean en masse! Grinding a handful of coffee beans
I enjoynthis time of not chasing this time of not being chased !

DEAR AMERIKA ! MY LOVELY DEAR SINGING CLUB
YOUR ENGLISH is as well … as YOUR SPANISH still ?
SAVE the WORLD and let's make AMERIKA bright again !
WE have AMERIKA so viel zu verThanken,
it was in former times the land of ...
liberty and democracy and freedom
has been and UNBEGRENZTE Möglichkeiten !
Coke, Hamburger, Holywood, Rock'nRoll,
Michael Gordon, Noam Chomsky but not that WEISSWURST today !!!

Excuse Me, i had to say that to an autistic man who is six years follower and
he is a hard bucket to work at to make him mature !

Yes, i see this LinkedIn is only useful for the aim how to present yourself in
it, and get the wanted contact to interested and sameway professionally
familiar people in the cause how to be supported in those abilities you bring
with, and working skills you offer, it is like a kinda very good job market at
least, not an socialnetwork place for coming together, the way i present me
there is the way i would have success with the performance i show in order
to get better known in real circles of life ! I have to be responsible on what
to present with files, documents, proving the reality, and certifications,
nothing but that, they want to see WHAT do i want, and i may still also read
in the news i like, but it is a search for a future, nothing but that, this is not a
welcome dears, you are all welcome to join in !
Sothen it stays save for job seekers, it depends on what do i post to make me
a good cake every week, until that ONE and ONLY scout will find me ! I
will only bring posts to my deeper interests and to other journalist posts as
answer, or maybe something to introduce books once in a while, i know
when you realize to investigate what all happens in your perception, ...
NOTHING, but that is another pair of shoes. Like welcome, i ride a horse,
while you ride a camel, i cannot change the way of life, and while you cross
the Sahara with the camel, you also might be to lazy to orientate yourself
and end in the desert end, because you end in wishings to cross a desert you
don't know.

The wannabe doubts everything.
He sabotages working relationships.
He suspects colleagues without thinking.
He or she always puts on the same facial expression of horror meeting them.
He invades strangers' private lives, always portrayed as an innocent angel,
who supposedly only means "well". He or she is a deeply hurt person.
He or she just puts one foot in front of the other,
until they run after him and stand in front of a locked door,
from where he guesses how a break-in into their lives takes place,
with a flashlight in his hand.
He or she is an opportune hypocrite, plays with the voice of LSD,
but formally only speaks to himself, no one can guess from his voice
that he or she is playing a false game, will one day have to go back home to
the parents anyway, sleep in the back seat when they go on holiday,
because they will be sleeping with the teddy bear, and they know that the
door to a better understanding will always remain closed to them !

Where is the touch with reality!
What losing touch with reality means !!!
The perpetrators' polite bow is the fear that overshadows everything.
To the gods in white, like the chefs of food
They're all in a state of emotion. They kill out of greed and enrichment,
as if they were rummaging through their victims' laundry.
Those who do not respect life have not acted out of courage.
Those who lose their composure for a moment
because of a seemingly harmless bald head, greed becomes their undoing.
Those who shovel their way to the top in politics
are those who divide everyone, smear them with slogans,
only to serve their product in a different color.

It is less of a gain than a sacrifice, than a victory, because you have
mastered all the competitions in your life!
They say, when you get up in the morning...
"She doesn't like me" we sleep in the same house,
but she doesn't like me, it's completely fine,
nobody likes me anyway, I hardly like myself,
but I like everyone else even less than myself,
maybe that's the case with her too, maybe she likes me a little after all?

Does a single, undersexed mother think I'm ennobled,
just because she's standing right in front of me out of boredom,
who only dreams of the very next vacation,
the extension of her own home,
the new brand-name bicycles for the children,
wobbles on her high heels, touches me,
orders me to work, thinks I'm the sun,
but prevents me in her plush, jacket,
the chic black one, staring at me excitedly,
from DOING my WORK at this, my workplace?

The DEMOCRACY DESTROYERS - PEOPLE!!
populists are not "men of the trade" who spread illusions to distract from it
to render the office ineffective, to destroy the coalition,
there is no such thing THE DOCTOR invention in people's lives
who have nothing to do with the tax world of numbers,
who constantly wash their hands of guilt,
the bookkeeping is always done by women,
who can do it "off the cuff", with the doctor's oath straight out the door, kill,
and do it with the pleasure of "I'm doing it, but I'm so sorry!"

VOLUNTARY and INVOLUNTARY INTERNSHIPS – PEOPLE !

Do an internship at the church, as required by the authorities, and you are a
single parent, in the years that follow, everything you say is always from
strangers, the boss didn't care, year after year, how they liked it,
I did such "internships" countless times in my life,
how they always appeared to me as I passed by, called it bully,
so that they could say it straight to my face:
"Well, are you counting them all ?"
"Look, there's the receptionist sitting!"
"You can see that when she finishes the day,
who she'll be in bed with at the end !"
"Working as a prostitute would be a good option,
a lucrative business, if I can shout that in your face !"
and laugh about it, haven't said "things like that !!!"

In german way of seeing this...is that this treator for Child's Rape will never
again find his rescue place in THIS LIFE. This fireworker, in "Rescue"
that i do know, a handsome mature one person, who would never ever
confirm with a Child molester who finds his contract in his traditional job,
EVER ! NO RESCUE ANYMORE who rehire a fireworker
who pled guilty to raping a 14 year old girl.

We just know our history, and I know where there are people,
the downright weaker ones do bad things,
just because they are weaker, that's cowardly
and against this we are called, even if Europeans are bad
have a reputation abroad, to be a country, where children are violated
to become even louder, than this has to be anyway !

When you consider, we are all born by chance, and what we have become,
that is a matter of luck, and it is absolutely nothing to be proud of,
the pure coincidence, the happiness of living together,
and this one life together, where the positive outweighs the negative,
and why didn't they realize, what a shitty little bubble they live in,
that in their shitty bubble of hate, segregating themselves from this world,
and seeing every morning how trees grow in front of you, hearing the blues
about a world, do you want to fill these lives with hate?
If anything, it's only about one thing, rich against poor, poor against rich,
what does that mean when the water is getting scarcer,
and someone is swimming in money, when you say, "the boat is full!"
and someone has fallen off the boat in the Mediterranean,
then there is hardly any alarm, clear that "everyone is dead, no one is there!"
so let's raise our hands, and we stand up to those,
since there is nothing here but "hate", we will move out into the world,
one denounces our mothers, the second acts as a catcher in the rye,
stealing their children, the third then gives the child to those
who abuse your child, simply because they give them arbitrary laws!
A little rave against the right!

No beer for Nazis!!! So many beautiful and bright colors here,
and FUN and getting louder, hops and malt are far from lost,
we were born to love and live, every day is a new beginning,
because we are not afraid, hang out the colorful flags,
until it is clear that everyone is welcome.
Not a single sip it all goes down the wrong way!

Parents never had anything to say to each other, after the perfidious form of
child abuse, and abused the child's own child to intimidate him,there was
suddenly a sense of vainness, and silent agreement. All of a sudden,
"everything is done." The viewer says, "Good for you."one of the drunks is
crazy, the other drunk is helplessly ill, but the third hater suffers from it,
devil in the details, taboo comes to light. Miniature - cheeky and naughty -
some family constellations are like the spatial arrangement of horror around

a person, surrounded by a horde of members, who feast on their own flesh,
like cannibals, in a self-mutilating manner, a piece of their own flesh slowly
melting in the pan, and manoeuvring a victim for the rest of their lives
so that they would have to take on everything that they always hated in life!

Whatever think, the perpetrators go for it, bad conscience compels them,
they can no longer bear to play games for hours in the circle of neighbors,
where everyone has something different to say,
as soon as one of them leaves, they fall into a gap that can be overcome,
they don't know any children who shit, and then wipe it away again,
they don't have sick people who vomit, until it comes out of their butts,
every year they dream unsuccessfully, broad smile through white Christmas,
they just shuffle along in old age, their constant honey on their lips,
as if the constant fear of losing, the reflection, the years of fat,
and one day nothing will revolve around them anymore.

A so-called wannabe Viking, not a hero, more of a prepper, whose only true
way of dealing with women, like his brother, in my opinion, approaches
misogynistic behavior, suddenly tried to convince me via email that in his
old age he had started a new "relationship" with a younger mother. My
answer was prompt. After all these years of distant conversation, I finally
ended our acquaintance in a calm and fair manner, so that he immediately
understood that this was finally and long overdue, a final discussion, in
order to assess personality and to give him my honest opinion of him. Good
that I'm finally rid of him! What are you dreaming of? I played the lottery
again and lost, what do you think?

I know my way, but being alone feels far less hypocritical to me than having
someone around me, and because it feels so much better sides, it is not a
perceived loneliness. I get so much visible and recognize people, which
takes me so far away from the family that others have to know about it too.
It's like with the strangely woman met twice in Schleswig, she's 20 years
younger than my mother, but looks exactly like her, encounter with her is
always like meeting a horror clown.

I tell her that every time, and we are both very relieved not to have experienced the real mother in our hearts.

So far so good, all this on the subject of happy family life I've had enough of this macho country. That's why I just turn down the guys outside or step on the gas. If my food tastes better that way, and I stay true to my own life, they have to look for girls in younger age groups. At most, those are the ones who don't have any children and are described as "well screwed, just a friend" and are allowed to make big eyes. Have fun with your goggle-eyed darlings, they really make you happy all around, and your husband can really use that too! To each his due, German proverb.

Best wishes from elsewhere, Heike
Self-determination for both sexes,
with regard to reproduction is not a question of conscience!
Abortion is not considered a crime,
it is our body, for which we only decide ourselves.
Women's bodies are a beauty,
the protection and defense of which is a right of women,
for which women alone stand.
The fact that a woman decides for herself
about a situation with a child is connected with the pain and woe,
with the consequences of the use of violence,
with the maturity for motherhood,
with the way of forming her own opinion
about her life against external control,
against the power-grabbing misogyny of men.

Who else would have the right, under duress
even by the church to which he does not belong,
to hand over the lifelong role of father to the man,
to force him to endure permanent unemployment,
at the risk of receiving almost no pension?

Even if "one" sees it that way, the woman is actually capable of
getting her BIGGEST ORGASM without the man's fumbling hand,
through the power of her own THOUGHTS, so to speak,
she doesn't need a MAN to help her - HAHAHA
and she doesn't need "I WANT TO BREAK FREE!" hihihi

You can learn a lot by watching and remaining silent.
If you are honest, you don't lose things, but the things that lose you.
The wind never goes away, the waves will never subside,
your sails will never come down, I have a piece of cake left for you,
you would have any coffee from me, to enjoy what warm hands serve you!

Don't blame people for disappointing you, blame yourself because you
expected a lot from them. They expected you to do the same as them, to run
away from everything and everyone!

Create your own world that you can escape to when others don't understand
you, but always pay attention to the bonsai, it must be pruned even in
difficult times, and nurtured and cared for, treated correctly at new and full
moons, it must go through all these ups and downs just like you,
as you should every day, to help your partner up!

Always pay attention to the financiers,
like many other populists... the whiners when they don't like them,
the ones who refuse to work themselves, who deliberately disrupt processes,
they only work to fool the government, insult the population decadent way,
arrogantly throw an island wedding, plan the break in detail,
and then have to resign hypocritically -
it was enough for him to get early retirement !

The CHANCELLOR QUESTION arises again, and the ability of an alternative proposal to wear a Norwegian sweater, plus the offer to "go swimming" with the Greens, then everyone knows what to expect. MORALITY has spoken say, the old people, with the shriveled faces... with the loss of reality, triumphally...

"Those OUTSIDE with the faces, who would definitely not vote
for a worsened economy, through morality and misbehavior,
in the cloak of philosophical hypocrisy" they say with acetic faces
"We're not going to vote for THOSE OUTSIDE either !" WHEE …

Federal government takes into account !
On election promise: "I will abolish poverty in old age!"
Last but not least, wanted also abolish general medical care and
VACCINATIONS, then all problems of old age will actually solve itself!!
with a devised BILL "It is with satisfaction that I allow myself, so to speak
bill you idiots!" ACTUALLY LETTING PEOPLE FALL...!

I only mean being in a POSITION to face DEATH,
which puts PEOPLE in a POSITION to empathize
with the immeasurable SUFFERING of other PEOPLE,
due to ADULTHOOD If this EXPERIENCE OF DEATH
and natural PERCEPTION were to disappear,
there would be virtually NO COMPASSION among PEOPLE,
no HONESTY, PATIENCE to listen to WHY someone else is suffering !

For example it will be said,
"With a CV like that, taking advantage of a life-extending opportunity is
basically superfluous!"

110

Rape One! - Afterwards everyone asks about the boys, where are they, the little darlings, every mother asks herself that, not realizing that one of her boys raped a woman that night, wherever he was stationed as a soldier, he will do the right thing, they say. It's just that some people from elsewhere don't understand what the customs and laws are like elsewhere, when they hide behind their army, and believe themselves innocent because no court will bring charges, because soldier rapists are considered minor offenses.

Rape Two! - Relatives and their issues are not linked,
no abusive behavior should come to light in the family constellation,
so she can deal with it alone out there, without a roof or shelter, without shoes in the snow in winter, without a bed, without food, and hopefully no one who believed her in life when she secretly and quietly told him what was going on at home, it is better for those close to her to no longer give her protection and access to the family and to go to the dogs, and to drive her away from home and throw her out of the house until this "affair" is over, that a student from the parallel school class raped her for the second time. No one cared in her entire life!

Third rape! - The rape is over, and this time a trauma that will last into old age, the woman can trip up again later if she really falls in love, in short. The saying becomes significant: you have to start over again in life, sometimes aim for a different career direction, maybe move more often, even further away if possible, and doctors, equal opportunity officers, women's groups, therapists say I don't need therapy, in this case it is only recommended for the perpetrators, lawyers advise me not to have any more contact with my family and to flee as far as possible, never to return, instead of just staring into the devil's mouth like a frozen rabbit until he has destroyed me, who even from afar still manages to denounce you as an expectant mother and do everything in his power to steal your new born child from you in the confinement, because the devil knows that in this country, the Weimar law applies, that every woman's child is arbitrarily taken away by the authorities, and no lawyer has the authority to do anything against it, not even up to the highest court!

111

Flashbacks had subsided after years, they only wanted to knock me off balance about four times while I was walking, in short. I didn't need a shoulder to lean on, it's only good when it's over.

I didn't have any disturbed sexuality. I only had one man for once-in-a-lifetime good sex, and that was nothing else, the rest I took into my own hands as I got to know myself, learned to think positively, practiced deeper meditations and physical cleansing. This was mainly just about the fact that I had to regain love for myself, which I managed to do.

Trauma is no problem, I know my inner anatomy, healing methods, athletic flexibility, dream work, working with people in crisis, dealing with bullying colleagues at work, single parenting excluded as financially disadvantaged, responsible interaction with weaker people, my strong tendency towards humor, tears, emotional strength,intact inner dialogue,able to set boundaries. Triggers revealed my innermost fears in dreams could not frighten me, rather just a former tremor of a primal feeling that lies far in the past.
IT'S TIME TO ILLUSTRATE, there are no monsters out there on the street who attack women, rather completely normal people, as it seems, but it is the perpetrators who are not seen among them. But they are permanent monsters in women's memories, because the perpetrators do not serve a sentence, as if the perpetrators did not even exist in society!
The worst church contributes to this is to stigmatize rape victims and discourage them in the worst possible way, in particular to re-educate them, even to the point of suicide, so that the victim is also to be driven out of resisting all fascism for the rest of their life and fighting for their own point of view! It is plausible that in rare cases, defense leads to the woman having the same strong resistance.

The abuse of one's physical superiority, therefore, abuses the view, the coercion, which triggers the shock that a woman could have defended herself in the same way!

The sexual assault
on a female person, as the GREATEST FORM OF HUMAN BARBARISM
is comparable to that of a physically strong person
who throws himself at her in such a way, beyond the necessary distance,
in connection with violence, hence sex as a result of violence,
so the superiority and threat is overwhelming for the woman,
in the acceleration of the act, she can hardly defend herself in the same way
as the animal that corresponds to the man,
because she is not the ANIMAL in this situation, so it is plausible
that here defense in rare cases leads to the woman having the same strong
resistance. The abuse of his physical superiority, abuses the view
the coercion that triggers the shock,
a woman could have defended herself in the same way !

Distrust of the population !
The problem is not that the population does not understand politics,
NO - but that there are still politicians who do not trust the population,
that they understand the best solutions best of all,
but they just do not trust us all to do it ! yet they stand up in front of us as
supplicants and at the right moment they turn away, quickly get into the
Mercedes Benz, and the supplicants are off and away, to beg for votes again
tomorrow, but shout out loud against poor people !
Democracy a 400 YEAR old building,
an old man elected, mentally diagnosed, rapist,
prevented from that he didn't hear in this building there is no longer any
question of arguments, integrity or empathy ! The rogue state wants to
expand, it is regrettable and inevitable, as voted ! Nationalists may feel as if
their silhouette is visible from afar, standing in line around a grill in the
barren steppe, and in the shade at 40°C, and drinking beer with neighbors,
yelling loudly that it is noticeable but who is looking for company ?

I use to go down to a poor man, asit and speak to him in the same height.
I use to let him decide when to talk, let him the chance to ask me something.
I use to listen to his wish and help him, as i need once in while something.
I use to react and interact, and don't want to share this way of life.
I use to make him sure, as i am glad not to live in the street.
I use to have fun with the one, who needs to push me with humor.
All this because i'm able to tell someone,if i am in the need to recieve help !

I say, the only way to realize what is REALITY, seems to be said, WITH
THE SPIRIT of the UNDERGROUND and POWERLESS against the
POWER of the mindless ! uhhh like my dream was shocking me about the
HELPLESSNESS of the OLDEST and WISEST.

Imagine that HELICOPTER PARENTS give children names
that exclude them... for example Armin, instead of Marvin
for example Alterfalter, instead of Malte
for example Nele, instead of Heule, example Eliza, instead of Be quieter!
for example Keike, instead of Heike, example Jörn, instead of Teddybärchen
for example Natasha, instead of Alihandra, no matter now...
princess is called "psychotic" by mother when she talks back, tumultuous
scuffle, shouting spoiled to be a nasty little one by the littlest ones.

Love is not divisible ! After I left America for expample, it became clear to
me that love is an ego, illusion of love, a subjective desire, not even a
thought, and what destroys all of this are things like gold chains and money.

The sun shines too brightly to fall in love with a beautiful face, the abyss
behind the facade goes deep. Many took advantage of love like having to
have things, something like dusty trophies on the shelf, but love is not like
owning things, You lose things and it means nothing but love cannot be
shared. The friend, would better know a naive way, networks deliver no real
communications, maybe a romantic past phenomenia reaching out to the
first beginnings, but it is not true, try to accept it. All other ways are the
search for romance, or a better world in a fairy tale, then abuse others in

presentce deliver all, to feed the consumers maniac hunger for more.
I have counted 73 types of people in the last years abuse my kindliness.
I will present lesser in english, only costs money and nerves. By the way i am not willing to apologize socialize in things like this. I see it has never happened that one learned my mother language. I just felt acceptance, as I have tried to be polite to almost everyone to do studies in the other language deeply deceived and ghosting and laughing at my efforts and at least left it anyway. The liars are easy to spot from a distance. I am no longer willing to play the acrobat for strange requests.

You have just to think about, thought maybe leave their technic, won't give a chance. What ever searching for support, and try to get in touch to people help me to find a scout for my books, but this is all ART work, might be just a tiny chance to success, where more business freaks handle things out, and more the prominence and studied privileged people, i would love to read their news. But i know, before buying something, always think about the practical use or better success you would have with it. Before giving own goods who belong into your hands, think about each person before you let them steal the things out of your hands. I believe that nowadays the Art world changed to an illegal stealing and robbing of wisdom all kinds. That the mass of worlds through years were all good stoff to build up other people, who push me out their ways, bully, trigger, fear me, leave me standing with empty hands, ghosting, delete my followers, and reaching the people, collecting stoff, then laughing and let me feel abused in trust. They even still call back, in order to ask for money or more.

It was definitely clear, all what i heard and saw, and almost smelled the dead fish ashore. So i stood in San Francisco ashore and in the middle summer heat, with family and the kids, saw the dead end of an Image, swimming left fish, in a huge tourist town, with the eyes on prison Island, and thought, this is all what they left ?

Auf dem Kieper

Who jumps at it, if they are simply polite in a foreign country?
Who quickly loosens up their way of thinking,
if this insight is enough for them?
Who forgives the other person, if they have already left you?
Who plays biological, if they are really more psychopathic?
Who gradually suspects that moving into society,
if they have chosen the wrong path?
Who imitates the marriage ploy, if their goal is only little girls?
Who has unsuccessfully dreamed of being a lover-boy,
if their mental state is laughable?
Who has no longer any leverage, if they lack the supple legs of a woman?
Who won't put their feet out the door, if official is looking them in the face?

Soul is lost piece by piece.
You believed so young that the world belonged to you.
Soulless but fresh out of your first love.
You were able to gain the power of money at the beginning.
Pieces of soul, your pride and dignity are lost.
You let it be taken from you and allow it.
Souls that never surrender to you, no admiration.
You wanted them to worship your body.
Soul catchers who throw you to them to eat.
You see a lie in it, it is the pain of lying !
If women would kill men, because they peed on their toilets,
the world would be a lot cleaner, the pigs that fly out of windows,
who have been disrespectful to women, would,
would, in short, be "more appropriate!" who play the role of sisters to them,
because they can't get it up without a little brother,
stand at the grave and breathe a sigh of relief !

FIGHT that holds you down WITH THE SPIRIT and POWERLESSNESS
against the POWER of the mindless about the HELPLESSNESS of the
ELDEST and WISEEST.

Every 4th man in the country is a customer who goes to prostitutes !
None of them knows why they are despised, abandoned avoided by women.
Everyone claims that it is their dream to heal a prostitute.
Everyone tells them to their faces that they "CHOOSE THIS PATH"
was her "DECISION" - and "That's how you wanted it."
They always wanted to cling to someone who, unlike the Madonnas,
would be there for them forever. None of them knows why they all think
they are degenerate, why nobody possibly liked them !

EVERYTHING OVER THE RIM ! He plays the conscience of the nation
for us from cloud nine down so high Mr.X, a sex-positive fuck philosopher,
society must stay outside, because only HE has "ideas"
he doesn't want to hear any of us, fenced in by intellectuals,
he laughs maliciously in the face of the "rest",
plays the Supreme Court while drunk, in 4% elite champagne,
at Sunday morning pints, because only he is the chosen one,
his self-loving thin broth, just like that on TV, irresponsibly ranting,
but it drips so beautifully "pregnant" out from the sauce-dripping strands.

Stupidity is a more dangerous enemy of good than evil. Evil can be
protested against, it can be exposed, it can be prevented with violence if
necessary, evil always carries the seed of self-destruction within itself, in
that it always leaves at least a feeling of unease in people.
We are defenseless against stupidity.
- Dietrich Bonhoeffer - Resistance and surrender,
letters and notes from prison

Wrong recommendation ! I have been observing for thirty years
how the writhing eel at the weekly market prepares to allow the base of the
people before the election to make no backbone statements,
no journalistic opinions, no recommendations for better politics,
no advice for the future, hence the image at the market of the "Writhing Eel"
it has nothing to do with a LINE that rolls through the salt, more with a
CATFISH that, seen in the DEEP, only feeds on the dirty mud !

Naive people are easy to abuse. Their male update of sentimentality.
The star is a god of a perfect world.
Despite all the hostility that everyone encounters.
The clearer the message, the more likely they are to give in.
You just believe and have to give in. You listen to someone in the spotlight.
Whoever made it public. A seducer is on a par with the Messiah.
It doesn't matter whether the local band doesn't really know the truth.
When the musicians puke behind the tent every night.
Their empathy is that of a grain of rice.
They are indifferent to their confrontation with death.
They only tolerate the sight of a woman with a microphone.
Because they want a woman in the stripper dirndl milieu.
And everyone sleeps in the dirt during breaks.
But they still make the boys believe for the local crap,
as if their friendship was great, that they come from abusive homes,
and pass this on to others, that their faith is deep and deserves recognition,
because they are affected by world events !
Folklore .. and just jumping to the same old record,
is like the way to cover up the confident, beautiful, funny, charming, gay,
now nervous and insecure without paying homage to outing yourself..
the fascists are looking for, they would rather bring the lying history to light
than the real problems,..you can relax so nicely..

Ohhh i felt totally better, to have binded pages with all my anger about
rapist and bullshit, but i agree this was specially better for me to have much
„fun" with it. I have always known in my life, I was the one who never
would need therapy as victim of rape, but the treators do, that's a fact, and i
make my way !

These days are not easy for none, the more the people become violent, the
more handsome people must heal and work to become peaceful and
unharmed by themselves.

A friend said, "You have to live your life and stay away from snakes. Live your life my friend and stay away from the things that make you miserable. Every day the sun rises you should enjoy it. Stay away from things that hurt you, because you won't benefit from hitting the water unless you get wet. He is looking for peace and security. Choose a friend who will take care of you and you will take care of him."

That is how i love always, too, likewise i am loner i advise the people out there do it like me. As well as i am an age, when the time to find trust in people would take to long, and more older people are, the more hurt they are from life. That way our chance to change life to a prickle champagne, i think is over. We all know about all those snakes, and fakes, and if sick people search church or anyone to hold on, they may do it as well, they need the support. The sick people are not able to save themselves, they even embrace all of it not to be confronted by themselves, without knowing their fate. Some are living in a selfdestroying circle of life, to be lead by the other, and believe naively stranger would do all their best for them, it is the most conveniant ways to live in a selflie, and follow the other every day. People with a mental or psychic handicap impossible to get out of that. Physical handicapped people often are far better in knowing what they want. I have tried that so often and so many times to explain, unsuccessful.

I am a woman from another cultural region, i wont't in this age try to make total changes of thought or believe. I am hopefully seeing, that you feel home with your believe. It is and was always my credo to get to know this place, that i may reach with my legs to go, and that i learned to fly in my dreams, that made me believe, that an airoplane flight to the moon destroys all knowledge about yourself, because to use only a machine and technic in order to become wise, is in my eyes another illusion.

I was outside with Mable in darkness and rain, but it was awesome ... it is the year of the dog Mable, all those Babies are happy to get to know her, this cuddle monster dog, she has such an empathy, at home the most time asleep, even the small who start to walk, all even the muslim Babies.

All touch and touch her, astonished minutes long, some start to cry if we leave sooner or later, so much inspirated by the caress of her smooth hair, and she always stood straight and does NOTHING, the more greatful patient or relaxed my dog is, the more babies love her this year - it is the year of my Philosopher Mable ! Today was a mom with two daughters, all three so flap and tumbling along the way, that i asked if they would be all sooo much tired ? Mom said, they had already longtime walked in the rain. So stood we and it was time for two young babies again make knowing my dear Mable. And caress and caress, and caress no words, only stood and the eyes of the both were pretty in a tumbling dream, how babies look when they are tired in the need of a hot bath and bed, but with Mable for that time stood still. I said to Mom this year it is more the dog with all babies of the world, we spoke about the cat we had. We spoke about the mice we had before, and i said the dog lives longer than the cat, the cat lives longer than the mice, and asked the babies, "And now what do you think how many dogs would fit in your Grandmommy ? Imagine this !" then the girl answered truly "Oh, no, i don't think any babies would ever have fit into my grandmom !" the Mom aside and i laughed out loud, that the babies could not imagine where the babies come from, and i only said "Babies, without the grandmommy you all would not exist !" this was out of her understanding, the baby could not follow.....hahahah

My abstract thinking, far from the stereotype, no, I only wrote the last enraged volume because I was fed up with the rape against me. I suffered with the politics of these days, worldwide too, and I had to put it into words that good citizens of this country like me, were not trusted by those at the top. But now everything is fine, the anger is gone.

Make sure you understand others before asking them to understand you. Most of our personal problems are caused by the gap between what I mean and what you understand ! If one day you lose the place of the seeds you have sown, the rain will tell you where you planted them. One day you will realize that you wasted the most precious moments of your life improving your image in front of eyes that only see what they want to see.

Money, the past, people...If you let them control you, you are lost.
I don't share things... Either I own them or I leave them to others..!!
My son, I give you some advice, heed it. I have met many enemies, the
worst of which are those who claim to be my friends. We suffer a lot when
we cannot describe what is inside us. Life doesn't give free lessons to
anyone, so when I say that life has taught me, rest assured that I have paid
the price. Your life situation will change if you change your approach to life.

OVER SEVEN CLOUDS ! A wrongdoer you can only do it as a person
affected bring to heel, you will care about everything clear in connections,
who were there then it's no longer a trauma, finally he has reached the
bottom, fell here like a stone, who wanted me there all my life, for him
lowered, inclined, low, low-lying, submissive, despondent to end up on the
rope, now he is judged, wished him death. He lives in the distortion that a
young woman is unaware of her feelings, a young woman is only obsessed
with sex, a young woman lives in a kind of self-presentation, she seeks
attention, she only makes herself younger than she really is.
That is a lie, for which he punished her, also as a stalker,
and in every way that presented itself to him.

I once walked down the street at night,
the path was long, as I lay there,
and yet there was someone there, I could already see him,
where was he going, I fled again,
the street is not a nice long hall,
slept on the edge of the forest,
next door a nuclear power station,
so I once lay on the gravel path,
and was always happy in the morning,
whoever looked there to see me,
was a person like you and me, he was first of all part of the team,
and I was alone, and he was welcome on the team !
Oh, when someone goes on a journey,
how good laughter is for everyone !

JUST BE COURAGEOUS !

Donna Madre Mia, porca misera !
I already have wet dreams, all the marks on the legs,
they already gave me all their foam, and I still see them today,
the plums swimming, while their erections combed the waves,
they were the sharks of the South Seas, all fighting for my little heart,
I'm still hanging in the hammock, in Uruguay, dreaming of the island,
that offers me a harbor, with the savior of my heart,
who brings all his friends, to share LOVE with me,
after traveling the Seven Seas, preparing the meatballs,
and offering me wet dreams forever..........!

ISLAND EXPERIENCE !
Good joke, the joke lies in it,
first I had to walk from the island
over to the forest, when I got to the end,
there was a food temple,
my mother was eating,
my sisters were snacking,
my father's puffed-out cheeks,
after I had searched for them for about 4 hours,
so I found them again at lunchtime,
there was nothing for me,
and from then on, for me it was just,
I had to step on the gas to be noticed,
run until the blood came out of my lungs,
think until machines almost ran over me,
and until I collapsed,
the trick is repeated often,
other girls have successfully and bravely told me this themselves,
I was simply AIR FOR THE FAMILY until today !
Is that your image of the conspiracy theorists,
of a "beautiful, perfect world"?

The summer will be hot, 30°C in November.
The reason for inventing air conditioning, can help the atmosphere!
The oil traders believe in God, with the goods he gave them.
They have no time to pretend that they have some form of
moral integrity when it comes to the climate!
New climate protection measures what do the developing countries say?
Climate protection has sunk, let's save ourselves the minutes.

THINK ABOUT, NEITHER EARL OR DUTCHESS !
Miss Sophie - "It's business as usual Mr. Pommeroi?"
Answer - "Yeah, toilet seats with lights from China, no more cheese from
Holland, flooded, good fracking gas is bought in Yellowstone Park
the collapsing developing countries are sending you thousands,
- NO - millions of climate refugees!"
Miss Sophie - "Fine, let them come. Then we'll save the world together."
Simply saying, "My dog is a bitch!"
what a little "bitch" she is, look, she wants to sniff very friendly
now look at that, completely friendly, well then goodbye, the little bitch..

Simply speaking, "We always look after her !"
what a nice little helicopter child she is
look, now she is developing depression from brainwashing,
no - scientifically speaking - tension - noise sensitivity -
MIGRAINES, as a result of the brainwashing !
but she will easily become the "desired bitch !"

ORGANIC MEAT in the RESTAURANT!!!
I'm craving COFFEE...was the animal happy, does it have a refugee history,
what about its lineage, does the farmer always choose "green"?
Oh, the calf is already dead? How can that be? Did it die happily?
Did it have friends in its region? ....is there a good Italian wine to go with it?
does it taste better than that of a conventional refugee???

Car dealer VW says - no innovation, no focus on the future,
but already digital rip-off, or invented hybrid, junk cars overpriced,
what is happening today - 3000 employees across Europe,
more people back on welfare, for wind turbines and kindergartens,
because they say - "Problems are just thorny opportunities!"
now people, "You idiots should still buy VW!"
 I'm working out "ALL THAT'S MISSING THE WORD FOR SUNDAY!!"
Car dealers as unpopular as the church, exploited skilled workers, random,
arbitrary layoffs, despite the need for more employees, exact same level !
It was a shitty year somehow, that someone jokingly wished me a good and
better new year, that has never happened before in my life! Thank you very
much! I think to myelf much more, but they still wished me "enjoy it!" hoho

Who are you ..?

I am the bad person who gets good from you if you think well of him. The
matter concerns your mind and not me. I am what I am and you are what
you think. The sea says: I am not a traitor. You are the one who entered my
depths without my consent. Love does not mean taking someone's heart...
Love means creating a place where no one can get you out.

To understand the suffering of another person, you have to swim in the same
sea in which he drowned. I know that, and I remember the depths into which
I got into, from which danger one can only escape by making exceptions,
somehow I had a guardian angel, and he laughed in my face!

Chi sei ..? - Io sono la persona cattiva da cui ottieni del bene se pensi bene
di lui. La questione riguarda la tua mente e non me. Io sono quello che sono
e tu sei quello che pensi..

I don't think I'm bad. I'm actually a pleasant person. I know myself better
than I know you. For me, you would only be the good person that I think I
see in you. I know that you are only as good to me as I think you are good,
nothing else.

Personal smell. Accept your own smell.
Be real - at this time - it's time!
Don't go out covered in make-up, you look like a clown,
but the bad kind who wants to show himself as if he were a butterfly !

Teach children early on that natural behavior is frowned upon,
of course some people learn in old age, because life has taught them,
of course everyone would know a solution to control their own pace,
of course they are wise from experience,
the humorous dress rationally, of course all dear children
must use the same tone together, if that doesn't work, a shrill tone, a war cry,
a stumbling step, and if it smells, an unfriendly look into the distance,
an "I don't dare do that!", an "I'm just making life difficult for someone"
because I know how to do it....! Just look at the country bumpkins !

They're sitting around unemployed.
They're getting rounder from snacking.
They don't have much of a clue about colors.
They spend the whole day knitting something.
They make sweaters and pashminas in the colors of their competitors,
never say where their children come from,
must have been the stork, ... But they say
THEY HAVE A HUGE UNDERSTANDING OF TEXTILES!
I never had to imagine, when someone looked at me,
what it might smell like, when I sat down on the desk chair, as always,
the boss covered it with silk, so that I would never move from my seat,
in all my work, and on the way I was to obtain it,
and when he was finally inside me, he said
"Now you will become him, you can count yourself lucky,
that God was inside you !" I then promptly gave back the key,
claiming that this workplace was far too expensive for me !

Nooooo, honestly, who wants to let the boss wring out the mop first,
and then have to sing him a song at Advent, while he wants to scan me
on the scanner, plus do a quick job on the document shredder,
just backwards over the reception desk, in from the side and then into the
next room, so that I appeared to him practically naked like a zebra
in every doorway? Yes, but I knew that was all he wanted....
I almost punched him in the face for that!!!!
But since I know that I don't have Bruce Willis with me but his Tina Turner,
I miss him, I can't even bring his baby milk anymore, I'm supposed to have
read somewhere about descending into the catacombs where I see famous
people who have died again, I don't even have to walk around the Kaaba
three times to see that I've gotten older too!

I don't owe anything to anyone!
What does an informer do when he is alone?
Stomping his own wine barefoot, or not using gender at all,
casually drinking half and half cherry and banana,
writing angry letters to the newspapers, feeling unfairly treated,
being a lonely man who was it, because he stole the queen's child !!!

Dear Angie! It is what it is,
because a man was fired once by an East German woman,
that he wanted to do EVERYTHING to buy her position,
even after 50 years, finally to make his career.

Dear March!
Your career was always as if it had been eradicated!
It is your personal P-OST TRAUMATIC stress disorder,
and WE understand you, now you will hit back,
we still don't like you, who are deeply hurt men,
who are extremely unfortunate in their kind !
And we know that YOU would do everything to
tread the hopes of all this country through the mud !

There is the theory, that 1871 downright invented by man,
who one day realized to be 1 man for several weeks,
who would know better how women are doing...
that today with it the conservative church direction
for women in 2024, it's real there is a lack of atheistic commitment.
Can it be, that you still have a man there HAS TO SPEAK UP?

Have U ever heard about that politicians think
about our society standing for their daily survival,
hotting from job to job, and teachings everywhere,
fighting for our good going for our kids,
trying all to bring the kids worthships,
really exercise all days and nights, with withstand against the evil,
and help each other out as good as it gets, that the conservatives hold us
for the "STUPID and LAZY CRAP"none would ever hand out work at last ?
And now want to force us to bow, and be ready for slavery ?
This for a better athmosphere in GERMANY !
Like politicians everywhere. Money-grubbing scumbags.
But own no selfworth themselves, as if the grubbing of money for them,
would fill the hole in their head ?

We just see it all decades long... the one missed his place in politic, he / she
leaves a hole, not very easy to see through, then the next leaves tricky the
even bigger hole at least, and leaves because unwanted, maybe we all say,
nowadays works once the unwanted want to return ????
Some people find it quite good, instead of laboriously searching for
mushrooms in the forest, they find one or the other in the swimming pool.
If you haven't used Tinder yet, you'll be wondering who you can push into
the pool today...? And which cheeky girl, will dare to do a threesome today?
Or try a fivesome? Perhaps too afraid of a tensome? The friend from the
street asks you if I come swimming with you, But don't pay attention to all
the men! I ask him before diving, can you do a crawl?
Everyone talks about the before sex and what it all means.
Who admits what they perhaps really wanted after sex?

Goodness,
the chaste girl gives the guy outside, a squinting look downwards,
sending the signal, "she's ready now!" not forgetting that he had the key to
her locker, not the one to her heart, nor a key, and for the second guy her
chastity belt wouldn't matter, because she would have understood !
Some children at heart try to express the variety of colors of the rainbow
and their tolerance of LGBTQ families in such a way that heterosexuals
themselves, in order to belong to the love, say they want to join in... simply
BECAUSE - "WE ARE ALL HERE, AFTER ALL, BECAUSE OUR
PARENTS DON'T LOVE US!" The LGBTQ family has a LOT OF
COMPASSION in such cases!!!

They have a really good "use" for other mothers' children, even those that
have hatched straight from the womb, unmistakably including abuse, the
question to the mother, giving her a little help, "You don't really want to
dream that people like you and your child are actually aiming for a career!"
and it has always been used, a stick up the ass and so on, to help the child to
recognize early on that it is a benefit, what is it doing with its mother...
"Where am I going to get a child now?" says everyone who doesn't have
one, so why argue with her... otherwise there will be a nasty situation, says
the STATE!

In the Cold War, there was still a clever recipe
from doctors to prepare for a birth... "Placenta Stroganov"
and if you prefer something from Texas, the "Placenta Smoothie"
that would also be an incentive for modern,
innovative obstetrics here to look forward to a German birth !
be a little more CAREFUL IN THE FUTURE when you enter hospitals !!!
Oh, no I still have it now too, forgot the hat... I stagger for comfort
buy a Börek, uhh, he's the lout, and at the fried chicken stand
but there is also sweating today...well, yes, where it looks like that,
if you have one or one, sometimes there is work, then they sweat.
I remember everything in my life !

COMPANERO The published version would have looked like that in fact, that i spoke in my talented direct short said all around the facts meaning way, about rapist, mind sick, misogyn, history and facts, the family, the army, the fairytale prince, liars, drugs, stupid cows, silly women, fuck to marriage, the church, the humanity of nowadays is really not mature enough to go through the truth, see the Artistic background of hand out my critics ! If people are warned of poisons in colors, no acrylic colors for my painting in pregnancy, never trust any childish crap from industry !

"If one said, I'm a one man sect no one would join."
Answer - no the opposite again, you may understand better, if you found a sect, then million followers, and you had not second rest of them all, you could never stand that. That is why all so many idiots tried to lock me to get in touch and present them my innerst sould that they would found that wisdom for their evangelic or even catholic sects they join, the purest and most authoritive asses, all want to be healers, promise me the peace on earth and in my soul, but first of all i had to trust them 100% and become therapy and in privacy and stop to talk to the public, they pretend to be coaches and psychotherist and studied, but none of their told crap is in 1% true, and they are someone else they show. If people fall is such dangerous activities act, they might suicide, with this it is easy to loose nerves. All wise people warn me not to get in touch with the snakes, it might even be the iciest coldest KI program.

1. Of all, it is important to them to be present in your mind with a photo that seems to match your sympathy.
2. most importantly, he speaks in a kind of portal with many other followers and not really daily known people from the street.
3. most of all he abuses all the stolen wisdom, enrages you and pisses off quickly with it no matter how you drown, but that wisdom they locked up for their purposes is there to abuse others and soon they spread the disgusting messages to the masses for a long time once one day they start reacting in the real masses of people and then the masses are manipulated.

I had some days long thought of a neighbourhood friend, who i don't meet often, he is very busy, and only had that name in my mind, and wups you don't believe there was two accounts who adore a seemingly person in the public, with exact that name, funny isn't it ? They really tried to get into touch, and would have chosen me with that use of the statistics.

Socrates says:
When I was young, I did not like to wake up early, and my mother hated this behavior from me because she dreamed of seeing me one day as a rich merchant..
One day, my mother went with me to the teacher and she had agreed with him to tell me the benefits of waking up early..
• Teacher: Socrates I will tell you a beautiful story and tell me what you benefited from it, okay?
• Socrates: Okay
• Teacher: There were two birds, one of them woke up early and ate insects and fed his young ones, and the second woke up late and did not find anything to eat... What did you benefit from the story, Socrates?!
• Socrates:
The insects that wake up early are eaten by birds!

Good okay, those ones who always like me are so stupid to enter the day early, and move, and act, and feel sorrow for friends, and suffer with them, that way am i the one who stands for, and those who stay laying down more until midday, would be the ones who let the world turn around their navel, but insist me to do all what i can ? This is a funny weird world.

And i understand with what you said, how about would it be possible to hide at any other place in the far world, with that knowlegde , i see it like that because a home land is a mother's land, so to see all of yourself in this land, and all over the places even the most greens and beautiful, would end in a days long party, but afterwards all those guestfriendliness would turn into a fiendly and they would ask me when to take the bus to find my way home ! Then friends here around in the neighbourhood are a treasure to keep.

This means no party, no meals invitings, no help the homeless, no accept the alcoholics, no tolerate the paranoid, no ask for warmth two houses further, no informate the wrong people about your friend.

We just came in for coffee, it was nice, the sun shone, birds across the fields, funny pairs with humor, and one funny talk about a young lady, that we both saw sometimes, she is a pretty pretty tall blond girl, got her man from a holiday through south america, where she went with a purse, a birth document, a passport and the credit card, to take the man with her right from the road, and took a street dog plus with her in the airo plane to this town, have an exotic husband by her side, always speaking about the nice travel in south america they had made, she put a magnificant tall tattoo on her breast i say the whole damn breast is a kinda djungel root and plant growing down to her titts, walking around showing that free wide tatooed breast for all to see. I am pretty pretty pretty sure these arrogant and vain people who play the exotic card for show so hard, won't have any children, because egoists have not kids.

When get to know her first time see her in her tattoo and shining bright like the sun,but in case i had already told her she impresses me not at all, how would her dog think he had to leave the continent, and home place inside of the loudest plane more than ten hours in a cage, and now slendering here in the lonliest somewhere else ? I say everybody who buys anything, even a husband and dog with the credit card, is in my eyes a costumer, not more than that, and a product for the show does once in a while loose the attraction.

In fact, "No one is free from worries," so he smiled. Money,the past, people, if you let them control you, you are lost. Hours fly by and days repeat themselves, but they don't bring back what they took from us. The pain is in discovering that you are just a passerby in a heart that means life to you, if no one'd give you the answer, that was to be expected ! If you need me, I'll forget the differences, be by your side as usual. Don't be afraid, I am not like you. The one who tried to be like you but couldn't will always hate you..

Love is a simple purchase for many.
Go to your favorite country, buy the exotic.
Go to your home country, and from then on just forget the loud airplane,
forget the home continent, forget the family, the motherland,
always talk about the story of how we met,
and show off your exotic car to the vain lady!
I'm lost for words, breasts are a kind of jungle root plant, that is visible up to
your tits, maybe next summer will be the next kick, get your stomach
tattooed too and walk around stark naked, what a load of crap !

Where does a person go when they feel
that not all places are right for them?
Love for us and happiness for others. There may come a time when
someone gives up everything to earn something, or what is left of them after
they have wasted it on bad decisions.
That is why it is good, also in view of the risk,
to walk on the rooftops, instead of like everyone else on the street,
to have seven girlfriends at the same time, to go in and out of strangers'
families, to think your own thoughts, and quietly play in a band, to travel
through the real East, to visit a mother in Ukraine, to lose your papers, and
still find your way home ! Life is not logical.

My life has been illogical. What I was given to eat was indigestible.
Today I say, yesterday it was gone. I cried my eyes out in the tree, the eagle
had the same feelings, and the eagle just cried with me his loud and long
song, of course I also say to myself, it sucks, when everything is taken away
from you. But I don't care about my soldier's boots.
I don't need a heart to fly at me from the side.
Nobody has to do anything the same to me.
Life is mine and mine alone. So I don't have to cry about love anymore!

After almost 45 years, meeting my mother's double -
I mean... if anyone needs all that,
I'm generous, you can choose what you want!

Get rid of the motivation to have children into this world !
If tomorrow is worse than today, people, then take your life, not so hard !
Just drive straight to the house, to the children's houses - avenue,
there behind the playground, take another turn, take one or the other with
you, and.... watch him grow wings ! I've just split up, now there's crying, so
the whole world should know, I'd rather hoist the sails, I say, nobody wants
to know about love ! Try to go through that twice, the first love falls apart,
as if you had stopped, you see him walking away, shaking his butt,
as if he wanted to leave you on the side of the road like a dog named "Tiffy"

Try to survive that a second time,
your whole life plays out, from the first misfortune to today,
you see yourself physically rearing up, almost exploding,
unable to do anything, then crying, all the way to the center of the earth,
then laughing to the highest peaks, and see yourself almost dying in the
process. If anyone thinks that I have become significantly more cautious in
the "love affair" since then. I only have one life!

PLASTIC WORLDS!
Which consumers... who eat the flesh of the defenseless,
are considered to be the 25% of brothel consumers.
Which language... no one can and should understand always drive around
houses, to ambush stumbling children, to catch them.

Which dragons... wait at the stove, at the edge of the bed,
but no one is standing in line anymore. No children are needed.
The old woman is already washing dirty diapers
when the customer returns home from his day out.
Do we pay attention to forests?
Do we burn them with nettle accumulations,
because of the higher nitrogen deposits.
Do we pay attention to women? Lost brothers, sisters and their fathers,
because of the higher destructive murderous companions.
Do we pay attention to German history?

We will not forgive like the Catholics, commit large-scale child abuse,
German history has taught us, "Those who look away, forgive the
perpetrators, give them church absolution, who still kill for base motives,
who perforate children themselves like cattle, for them no crime exists,
because there are no victims for them !"

If he makes a run for it, he always dives with his hood,
but he never needs diving goggles for his pupils when diving.
For this reason alone, I always refuse to greet old men
wearing hats or caps, because they have no good faith
and only wear the hood to scare others !
What if your fairy tale about the forest actually sounds like that? -

Over a mass grave that was dug deep,
a little house was built in the fairy tale forest,
there once lived a poor family, who were quite antisocial,
who, during a period of poverty,
simply dropped the children off in the forest,
but the children were also antisocial, they attacked and broke into houses,
just like that, to survive, the people from the village, the locals,
but out of anger they burned the old woman in the little house,
on the grave of the buried people they had once shot in concentration camp,
on which they first built a meadow of herbs, later a field of nettles,
then another hut, which served as a tourist lookout point
in the "New Fairy Tale Forest"!

If he makes a run for it, he always dives with his hood, but he never needs
diving goggles for his pupils when diving.
For this reason alone, I always refuse to greet old men
wearing hats or caps, because they have no good faith
and only wear the hood to scare others !

Those who look away, like those who rely on the fact that forest floor
remembers the things that happen in it,
like the skin of small children, is that true, even they deny it,
until they are old, grey deniers and perpetrators,
who to this day make excuses, repress guilt, wash their hands of it,
preach table prayers to children, who mistake water for wine,
dig just a little deeper under the ground, to get rid of the corpses of those
who they chased to their deaths, including their children,
they must hold themselves accountable for the rest of their lives,
because nothing of this kind expires !

It hurts to walk by the wall, avoiding problems, and then the same wall falls
on you.

A woman walks along, picks up someone out of pain,
he stands up, but without really noticing her, leans on her like a stool,
knocks it over, and even kicks him, and the dear woman realizes
how little value her love is in this case ! There's no point in closing the
window while the scene is still playing out in your head.

I still see the twin at the window. He sees the friends. He sees the brother.
He sees the friends with the brother. He sees the friends turning to him.
But he reacts paradoxically and takes his own life,
and truly without anything happening !

Your living room has bought up 71 pubs.
A financier has applied to be a bartender, what do you do?
I would show him what this meant "Real life !"
I would let him sleep outside in a tent despite his temporary work, live
outside in a tent with his babies mother, can't guarantee that the temporary
job will lead to anything more, to confirm to me how many women he has
already slept with, then I'll call him a son of a bitch in front of other people,
on top of that he can expect a lot of blows behind the bar, tips are given if he
works cleanly, his outfit has to be a cheap tracksuit, he can fill up nuts.

I had again a real big viking dream, as if the regional viking club welcomed
me in their midst. The woman asit told me why to drink always much, and
the man over there told me why such a husband man might be not the worst
of all, and i saw the snow and kinda little Upsala, the small houses in winter,
and they honored me to have the same way for breakfast. Now i know it that
i am not totally alone in this world anymore !

That it is time to count on yourself,
asking your own mind, how it would be,
to change the awareness into the fact,
that it might be to stumble and fall !
This credo is far more important
in order to finally once in life to reach
that no other waits for your help but YOU !

Just not in order to loose the believe in humans, i had surely found the
quiete right decision not to trust in a man anymore !

And here I am. As usual,
looking out the bedroom window and chilling my ass,
thinking everything to let my thoughts run free,
the feeling of hopeless passivity?
Then the only salvation is to free the mind from the body.
Just push it up and look at everything from above.
Sit under the ceiling lamp and watch.
Without being touched, sucked in.
He's been all over the world.
It must be a legacy from his mother. She was like a weasel
stay in my thoughts, fly in your direction, fly straight into the spring mill.
It's undeniably easier to let your thoughts run free.
I in that box anyway? Was dusty in there. But I want more!
When we were children, the same boundless, happy closeness.
I stay here at my post. And look at the seasons.
That it's damn annoying not to have braces!

How hard can it be to get me a pair? Or even a few.
A touch of nostalgia on a drunken evening? Loneliness, guilt?
Maybe the lack of childhood?
Maybe because I'm a symbol of the good that was.
He has always been a cheerful bastard, since I've known him.
He didn't have many friends at the same time, only one or two at a time.
Juice and rolls. Get it, it's good! Mmm, big boy...
But how could he still push me away just like that?
Hear them playing and dancing to Elvis, never understood what is about.
It was just an annoying hum. Among the other childish things.
Not much Elvis to dance to toda, the lyrics and that things are changing,
slow ballads on a brainless acoustic guitar.
Know that I've grown old and my hearing has dulled.
But I don't think that's the whole truth on the subject.
It's his life. Better to go to the ceiling light and climb.Watch what happens,
but without touching it. I will regain control of my thoughts. So that they
don't run away with me anyway. And burn up in confused, angry rage.
I only collide with things that make me happy. But I want to join!
What fun we will have !

Thankyou, my friend !
I am just happy about it, not to be lamed, and being stuck in a moveless
corps, sothen those people have to travel to their ceiling, and can't dance or
fly !!! I know that those people may think, and all those years being stuck in
daubts, fears, loneliness, distraction, wanting out ! It works out, until that
day is reached that they will land on earth as commod, balanced, artist and
thinkers, who play their role as handicapped with good emotion and humor
and travel in words.

Brunette seal pup
You are the match for all guys! What a quick short film?
Happy to leave fields of corpses,
and heaps of women on the way, just for someone like her!

You finally have someone who agrees to have real fun with someone.
The fuss about solidarity. The fuss about being loyal friends.
The gift tour and legwork is all just pandering,
every whore has had enough of fucking one day, and then
it doesn't matter, and learns to distrust and just be unknown.

I, blonde seal pup. I'm not into bad love!
I never leave corpses behind, and they pave your way in heaps,
just for someone like me, you didn't exist!
I don't have anyone else up my sleeve, if things don't work out,
she celebrates herself more easily because she knows
that she stole the guy from someone else.
There's enough fuss about assholes,
who give "gifts" and without any obligation
it's all just a show, don't give a bite for it,
it's not worth trying, trust, invite, and then let the others follow suit?

Philistines, as I now know, don't want to know me, because...
they can't tell me in usable bits and pieces,
that they hate listening to me snore,
that they don't like hearing me talk at all,
that they feel interrupted by me,
because they are concentrating on other things,
that they hate the hair on my floor,
because it reminds them of my dog,
that dogs make them throw up their coffee,
because they can't imagine me as a cleaner,
even though I have a nice home !
Sleep your way to the top, while you still can,
you won't always be fit, today an apple, tomorrow a plum,
no more scripts, the replay on the monitor, with spots and a double chin,
who likes to see you when you're fat?

Everyone got what they didn't want,
slept their way to the top, stole other people's partners,
no longer wanted to be fuckable, no longer wanted to get a role,
wanted to be the center of attention in order to get rich,
haphazardly looking for fun, that a child is as disruptive,
had in truth no more empathy to try that alone with a baby,
as an unsuitable film project, the festival isn't life,
why plan, in the end it all turns out differently than you think,
because the guest in your heart has usually already left before you,
you just have to clean up the mess you've created.

You can choose... a dealer knows that if it gets too hot for him,
foreign countries always wave a friendly hand.
A flat-rate sex dealer relies on it...even if it's sterile, the sight of children
never bothers him. While one...is always ready to betray you for a few roast
chicken legs. A dishonorable heartbreaker... is not someone who would
forgive a mother for her children, let alone for her love of cracking nuts !

Girl wants to belong one day. She finally doesn't want to be a clown
anymore. All the others go their own way. She lives in the belief that faith
lights her way. But she doesn't recognize the colors.
She puts so much effort into finding meaning, chooses the uniform and
looks up to them. Horrified, she loses herself in the feeling that she has to
help. But since everyone only helps themselves, no one hears.
Her cry for help goes through the roof. No complex is as painful as wanting
to help. Even if pity doesn't get her anywhere. Because no one surrounds her
with grateful love. She becomes the avenger of the corrupted,
the savior of the disinherited, the believing martyr, against all the injustice
in this world, opening the eyes of the unbelievers, so that they should
understand what love is, shooting everything "evil" in her mind.

My question, who is the treator ?

Is this the person who acts as martyr, even a woman with the believe to kill first in order to make people think of the better in God's believe ? Is this the one who acted proudly presented shoot several people, just in order to save his and his fellows life a treator with a trimmed life afterwards while do his job, and live another personality with no more speaking that he remembers his childhood awareness anymore ? Is this the perpetrator who leaves a nightmare mask in everyone, the witness of a sick person who kills and bullies innocent people throughout his life? Is this the father's heritage to his children, who walk a lifelong on the road of peace, that her father would do everything to set the seed of a killer into his kids minds ?

I see it like that, everybody may find the sense of life himself, if he apologized his bad deeds to the victims. As well as the truth may give him one single day on top of a box standing make himself feeling free for this moment, and see, that all his life decisions have been wrong ! Confrontation to everyone as treator, is his only chance to continue life, while the truth will one day give him back his sympathy and the power back to accept life. I mean that all human life only depends on how everybody learns to handle the emotional life each carries around, many because of that need help to carry the weight, the real enemy is always inside of the people to find, and to respect this awareness gives everyone the chance to learn from it.

THREE IN ONE GO ! Hardness from the one who calls himself socialist, describes the night after attack he simply confronts with ignorance.
HE MUST FIRST WALK BAREFOOT HIMSELF! Hardness from that, who scolds himself fatherly, talks about good schoolgirls, live in a risky dangerous world, but the student attacked the daughter, she is, was, will never exist in family! HE MUST FIRST HIMSELF FEEL HUNGRY ! Hardness from the one who knows that a girl would take her own life because of such things, but he wants to drive the daughter to the point she would shut up about his activities. HIM TURN OVER IN HIS GRAVE ! ... until he FEELS the HARDNESS that emanates from him!

It hurts to walk by the wall, avoiding problems,
and then the same wall falls on you.
He who is accustomed to playing the instrument
of deception will never master the melody of truth.

He who has just escaped a lie
and peacefully set his life straight
because his heart beat for the truth,
for which he fought with all his might,
is always testing himself and is...very,
very close to my soul!

143

144

145

147

148

151

152

153

154

155

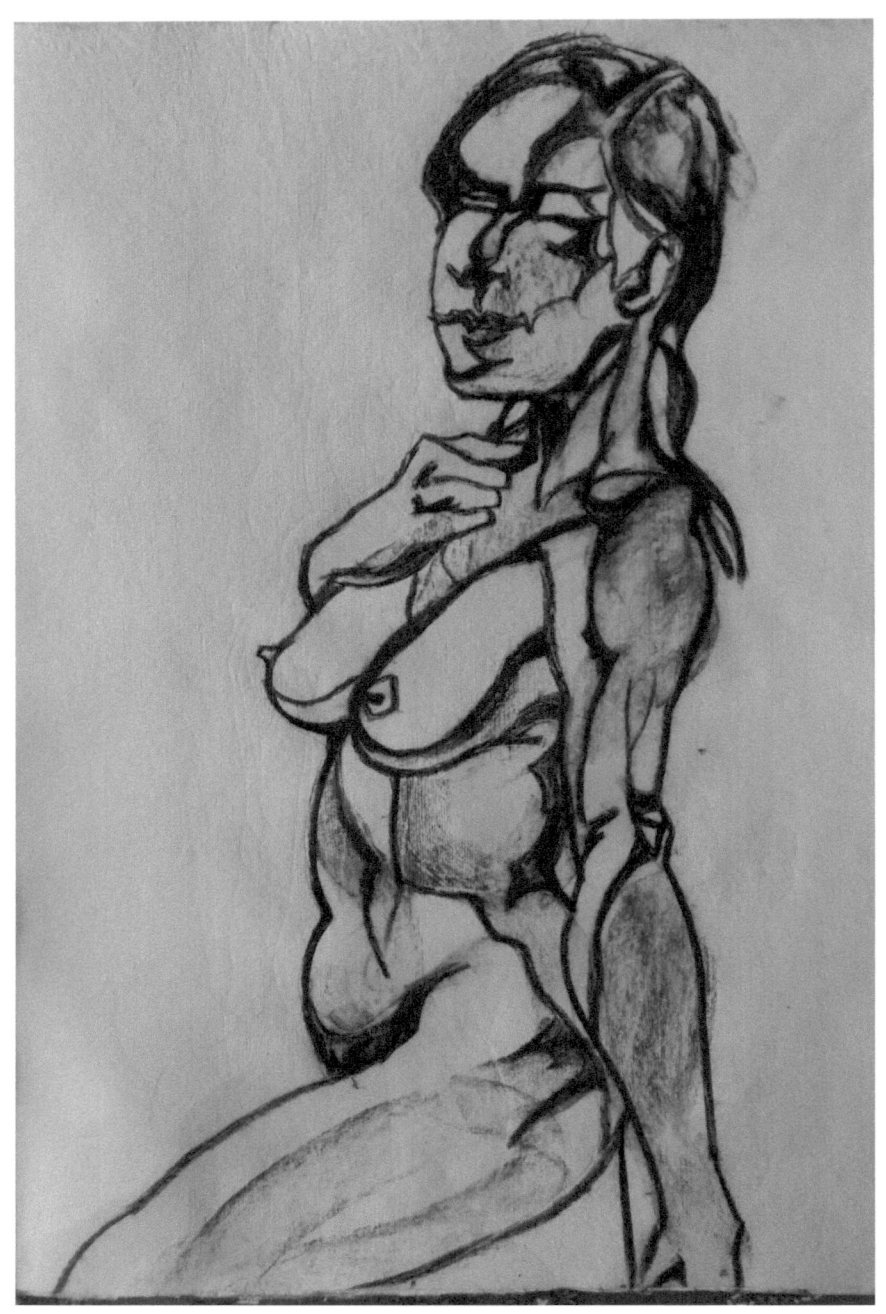

156

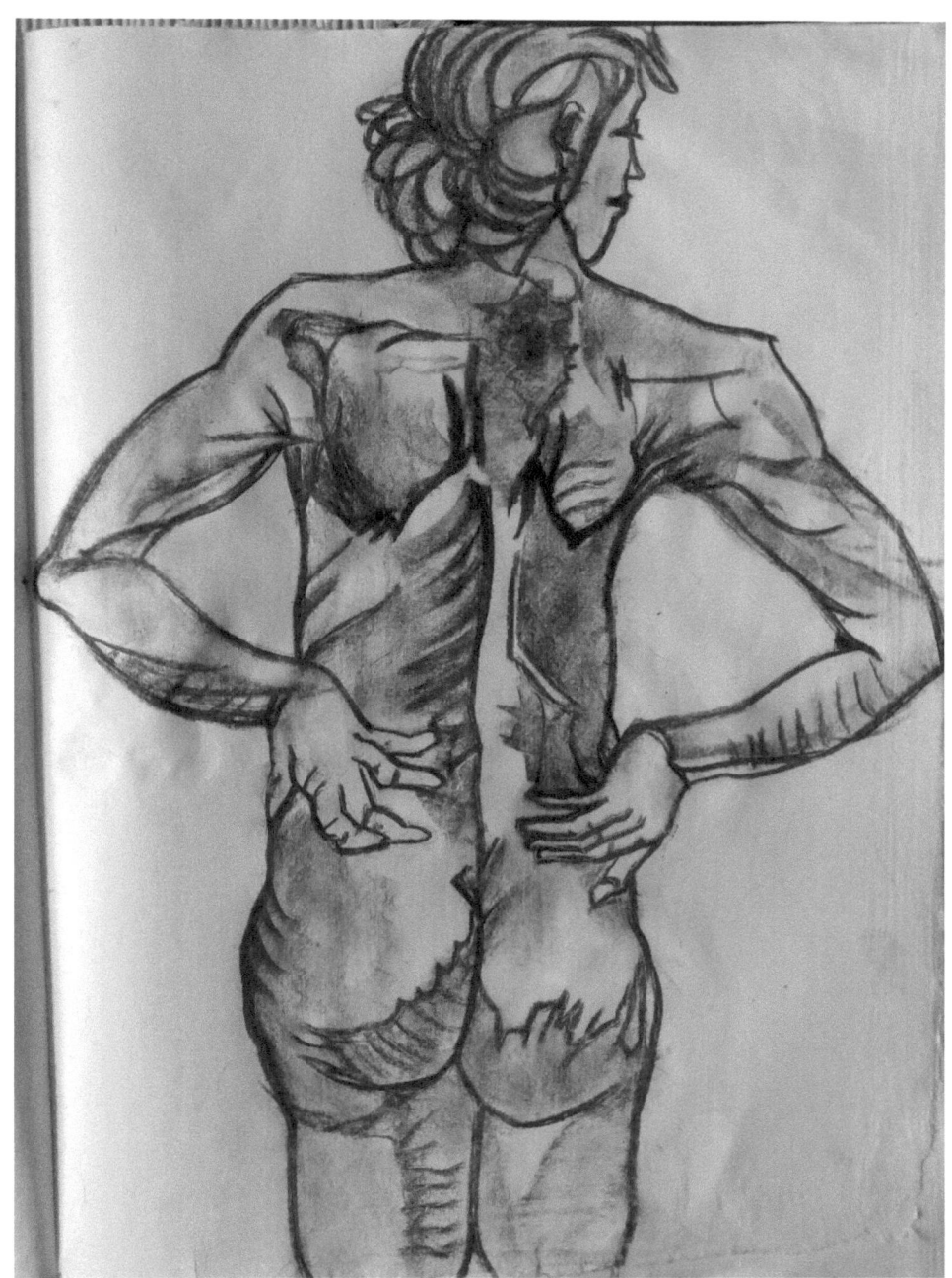

159